Praise for

CROOKED LINES

"Intimately candid, buoyantly human, and inexorably Jewish—Jenna Zark's *Crooked Lines* is all that and more. If you've experienced an unexpected loss in your life—or are merely preparing for the losses that inevitably come for all of us—you'll find Zark's book a heart-filled tonic filled with tenderness and humor. Just splendid."

—Paul Maccabee
Author of *John Dillinger Slept Here: A Crooks' Tour of Crime and Corruption*

"Jenna Zark's memoir, *Crooked Lines*, succeeds where years of religious school failed me. One holiday at a time, Zark examines Judaism and its rituals and demonstrates how Judaism provides structure, strength, comfort, and community to her life. Zark's honest and beautifully written memoir makes religious faith personal and powerful."

—Margo Weinstein
Author of *Jalan-Jalan: A Journey of Wanderlust and Motherhood*

"*Crooked Lines* by Jenna Zark is a little gem of a book. Writing as someone who had not grown up in a particularly religious household, Zark offers up a soulful, intimate look back at her life as a Jewish single mom, struggling, wondering what nuggets of wisdom, comfort, and grace she might be able to find in the faith of her foremothers that could help her navigate the challenges before her. The result is much more than a powerful personal memoir: it's a story full of such universal resonance that *all* readers concerned with the experience of single mothers will find the book a useful touchstone and guide."

—David Grant
Author, playwright, screenwriter

"Jenna Zark's journey through Jewish motherhood is unique. She opens the door to a world usually hidden from view, discussed in whispers, kept secret. As a writer, I stand in awe of her ability to illuminate her world. I could not. In keeping with the tradition of forbidding *lashon ha'rah* (gossip), Jenna lays bare her pain, confusion, and eventual reconciliation of her own heart."

—S. J. Schwaidelson
Author of *The Pomegranate*

"Zark seemingly effortlessly weaves storylines that are unique and universal at the same time. Her essays' rich, fluid style pulled me in long before I was a mother myself."

—Emily Cornell
Former managing editor of *TC Jewfolk*

"I'm not a single mother, yet Jenna's prose is so relatable in so many ways. She is striving to create a Jewish home for her child in challenging times, asking the same probing, difficult questions that all people—Jewish or not, parents or not—are asking regardless, every day. Jenna's story is proof that the journey from A to B isn't always quick, easy, and expected but is rewarding, nonetheless."

—Lonny Goldsmith
Editor, *TC Jewfolk*

"Jenna Zark has managed the unusual task of providing a Jewish holiday primer neatly wrapped up in a personal voyage of self-discovery. *Crooked Lines* holds the reader's attention from the first page, the author's story told with a genuine, oftentimes humorous, always hopeful voice."

—Caroline Goldberg Igra
Award-winning author of *From Where I Stand*

"As a Christian reader, I was fascinated to learn so much about the beliefs and traditions of the author's Jewish family, made even more poignant because she was going through her own exploration of her family's Jewish roots. In sharing stories of suddenly finding herself a single mother and navigating the rough, crooked road ahead of her, she hit on universal themes of love, life-changing loss, fear of change, and courage to face those changes that happen, in one way or another, to us all.

—Elizabeth H. Cottrell
Author of *Heartspoken: How to Write Notes that Connect, Comfort, Encourage, and Inspire*

"In a world where people joke that Jewish holidays are all the same—'They tried to kill us, we won, let's eat'—Jenna Zark puts the life back into the Jewish calendar. Each of the holidays in the annual cycle give structure to the events in her life, and her life gives meaning to the cycle of Jewish holidays. Every holiday is a gem, and every chapter is a gem. Life happens, and together with the holidays on our calendar, Jenna helps us envision how these holy days can make everyday life holy."

—Rabbi Randall J. Konigsburg
Beth Sholom B'nai Israel

"I highly recommend Jenna Zark's new book, *Crooked Lines*! Jenna's honest portrayal as a divorced single mom struggling to create a Jewish life rings true to me. She is honest and wise. Through her experiences, single parents will gain ideas to comfort and inspire them to find meaning in living a Jewish life. I hope clergy and synagogue leaders will read her book to learn how to better welcome single-parent families into their communities. I encourage single parents of all faiths to seek wisdom and solace from Ms. Zark's beautifully crafted stories of her honest struggles and spiritual journey."

—Rabbi Julie Gordon
Falls Church, VA

"*Crooked Lines* is a beautifully written book about a single mother's journey with life after an unexpected divorce from her ex-husband, a Jewish cantor. The themes are universal in that it talks about loss, transition, hope, motherhood, community, the power of rituals, and the many facets of religion. I often felt like I was reading poetry and would stop on certain lines and breathe in and out to really take them in for their beauty. A thought-provoking read, and I recommend it highly."

—Meredith O'Brien, LCSW
Author of *Opening the Door: My Journey Through Anorexia to Full Recovery*

Crooked Lines

By Jenna Zark

ISBN 978-1-64663-748-5

Published by

◤köehlerbooks™

3705 Shore Drive
Virginia Beach, VA 23455
800−435−4811
www.koehlerbooks.com

CROOKED LINES

A SINGLE MOM'S JEWISH JOURNEY

JENNA ZARK

VIRGINIA BEACH
CAPE CHARLES

*For Josh and Pete, who brought me from there
to here without breaking*

TABLE OF CONTENTS

WHEN A FRIEND ASKED if I wanted to write articles about Jewish life for her new online magazine, I thought, *No!* but surprised myself by saying, "Yes."

I never had any special insights into how to live "Jewishly"—the opposite, in fact. When my friend approached me, I think part of me wanted to write about what I'd been living through. I had an unexpected divorce from a cantor who worked in a synagogue, which led me to a path full of undergrowth, just waiting to trip me up.

I didn't have the first of idea of how to manage being a single mom. Nor did I know how to raise my son alone in a world where everyone I knew was a couple or becoming one.

And yet—*and yet.* I began to see the Jewish holidays and rituals I'd grown up with as a kind of anchor to keep me from falling flat on my face. That's where I started, and why I started. A small group of essays for an online magazine called *TC Jewfolk* brought me here and became the story you're reading.

There's a cheat sheet on the holidays and rituals at the end of this book, in case you want more information. But the story is *yours* whether you're Jewish or not, because we're all on unexpected journeys, aren't we? Stumbling along on crooked lines to get where we need to be.

1

SINGLE MOM SEEKS MEZUZAH

IF YOU'RE A JEWISH SINGLE MOM (who wasn't raised all that Jewishly), you already know the last thing you're thinking about when moving out of your old, married life is a Jewish prayer scroll (*mezuzah*). They are supposed to be mounted on every doorpost of your house as a daily reminder of Jewish identity. Is that why I was thinking about them?

It was late August, and I was packing up everything I owned to move across town to the bottom half of a duplex. My son, age four, would live there part of the time with me and part of the time with his dad in our old house. I had everything packed up and was ready to go to bed, only I couldn't. I was thinking about mezuzahs.

The day before, I told an Orthodox friend I was moving. She asked if I had mezuzahs to bring along. "I, uh, hadn't thought much about it," I said, which was only a partial truth; I hadn't thought about it at all.

"But when people don't have good mezuzahs, it's a problem," she replied. "In fact, it's the reason there is so much trouble in the world."

I looked at her and she looked back at me, and I realized she was quite serious. Though normally I might have nodded politely and talked of something else, the idea of a mezuzah protecting me from all the trouble in the world rang true. Because you're not only leaving home when you leave a marriage. You're leaving everything you thought was right about your life.

"By the way," my friend said, "those mezuzahs need to be *kosher*," meaning sanctified. "If you want, my husband can inspect them."

I smiled at her, trying to buy time before replying. I was moving to St. Anthony Park, hardly known for its Jewish traditions. My head was full of things I hadn't done and wanted to do, like getting a *sukkah* (temporary hut for the Jewish pilgrimage holiday called *Sukkot*). I was also trying to figure out where to put two sets of dishes so I could be, yes, kosher, or observant of Jewish dietary rules. "I'll find some mezuzahs and let you know," I said. My friend directed me to the gift shop at her synagogue, which I promised to visit.

Later that night, I thought about the mezuzahs I wanted and where to put them. I decided something ornate would catch my eye and brighten the house. The next week, I found what I was looking for in St. Louis Park; a friend gave me something as well. *These and the mezuzah I bought at my friend's synagogue are enough to start,* I thought.

Then came the inspection.

"Ms. Zark?" a man's voice intoned when I picked up the phone three days later.

He introduced himself, explaining he was my friend's husband. "Sorry. But only one of your mezuzahs is kosher."

Apparently, the pretty ones didn't have the right scroll or the right kind of scroll to be considered legitimate. "Can't I get some new scrolls?" I asked. My inspector was opposed to this idea and thought I should get new mezuzahs from his synagogue instead.

I thanked him and hung up, trying to finish making dinner and rid myself of all the horror-movie images suddenly flooding my mind. I couldn't help seeing a little newsreel of everything that COULD go wrong if I didn't get a truly kosher mezuzah on the doorposts in my house.

I want to tell you I'm not superstitious, because my parents always said Jews are not supposed to be.

But I'm superstitious. I am.

I looked at my son arranging dinosaurs on the kitchen floor in preparation for a war between the T-Rex and brontosaurus. Seeing his face, alight with the pleasures of play, made me want only to keep him safe, so the dinosaurs in his life are always small and manageable. Would a mezuzah do that? While I had grown up Jewish, I had never done much more than glance at the ones on my doorposts. Were they really so important? Why?

What's inside those long, thin containers? Mezuzah scrolls contain the first two paragraphs of the *Shema* prayer, commanding us to "write them on the doorpost of your house and on your gates" (Deuteronomy. 6:4-9). Jewish writings also say having a mezuzah on the door of each room means whenever we move from one room to another, we bring the presence of God with us in a way that sanctifies God's name. Because of that, some people touch the mezuzahs when they enter a room.

Fine, I thought. I know this stuff, but it's not something I wanted to deal with when I look at a doorpost. *Sorry, but no.*

Then I read something that made me want to read more. It said something about mezuzahs keeping away evil spirits. Not like the ones in horror movies, but the monsters in our minds and hearts. And having just gone through a divorce, I knew those monsters. They were persistent, real, and much scarier than an actual T-Rex showing up at the doorpost of your home.

Which meant I probably (okay, really) needed a kosher mezuzah. But what did *that* mean?

To be kosher, a mezuzah must be handwritten on genuine parchment. A specially trained scribe, known as a *sofer,* carefully writes the words using special black ink and a quill pen. The letters must be written according to *Halacha* (Jewish law). Every letter and word must be correct; any mistakes or missing letters invalidate the entire parchment.

I sighed, not wanting to give up my ornate mezuzah. *Could I get another kosher one and keep the pretty one?* I thought. *Maybe on a doorway underneath a kosher one?*

In the end, that's what I did. And I must tell you, throughout the year or two we lived at that apartment, I skirted no end of trouble—from carpal tunnel to money troubles to a heat breakdown midwinter—and all kinds of things in between.

When we moved to our new house, I brought all the mezuzahs with me and got some new ones.

I haven't seen my Orthodox friend lately, but if I do, I'll tell her I'm doing my part to keep all the trouble out. And on nights when things feel scary and I think those monsters are surfacing again, I still reach up to touch those mezuzahs. More than you think.

2
COUCH ANGEL

THE CLOSER I GOT to the holidays, the more depressed I became. Being a newly single mom who was recently divorced from a husband of thirteen-plus years seemed shaky enough; but having to move out of our first house together was worse. He had moved out temporarily while we sorted through divorce issues, but the house we shared was among the perks of his job as a member of the Jewish clergy. It was *his* house—not mine.

That meant I had to find a new place as soon as possible. The house itself was right across the street from the Mississippi River and offered large, airy rooms and incredible sunset views. I had once been extremely excited about calling it home, but at this point it made me feel itchy all over in ways I couldn't explain. All I could do was work on moving, staying sane, and trying to sell a couch.

Moving was going okay, but the other two points in my three-point plan were less successful. I have found that the more I need money, the less it tends to come my way, and that instance was no exception.

All I knew was I didn't want that couch to follow me to the new apartment I'd picked out for myself and my son. I wanted and needed to start fresh, even though I didn't know where my next couch would be coming from.

Instead of selling it, I decided to get rid of the couch quickly by giving it away. I called up someone I know in the Russian-Jewish community, and she put me in touch with a place that communicated with immigrant families. Within a day, a man speaking heavily accented English called and asked if he could come by. We sat on the couch together while my son played with his toys on the floor. The sun poured into the room, and I couldn't help but wish it was a happier occasion. Yet, the man told me something that added several layers to that day than if I had just sold the couch.

"In Russia, you live like wolf," he said. "You get up and all day you are just trying to get something—food, clothing, shelter," he continued. "In America, you have no idea."

I wanted to say *I have some idea,* because being a suddenly single parent is certainly no picnic. Still, I had found an affordable apartment with a fun little nook where I could work on plays and other writing. I also had an appointment for a job interview that week.

Listening to the Russian man's story made me feel better—at least for a while— about hopping out of the security blanket of my marriage. It also helped me realize that giving away your possessions can make you feel rich in a way that selling never can. I decided I would rely on the fates and hope for a couch angel to show up when I was ready to get a new one. Meanwhile, my son and I could use our floor cushions.

The Russian man and I said our goodbyes and I took my son to the playground. That evening, the man stopped by with his wife, Nelly—whose name I remember while her husband's I forgot. After just a few minutes of helping the couple move their new couch, she gave me a hug—and not a tepid one, either. A week or so later, she called and invited me to dinner.

I said yes instantly, thanking the universe for another way to connect to the world at a time when I was feeling lonely. I wish I could say it was a perfect dinner, because Nelly was lovely and funny and very kind to Josh.

Nelly's husband, on the other hand, brought his wolfish side to the dinner and tried to kiss me whenever his wife left the room. That made it harder to see them again, and I kept wrestling with myself about what to say if Nelly ever wanted me to return for another dinner. She didn't call me again, and though I did find myself wishing I had the presence of mind to kick her husband, I can't regret giving away my couch.

I suppose if the Russian family had shown me a perfect picture, instead of what I did see, I could have felt sorry for myself on the way home, thinking about my inability to find a happy marriage and wallowing in newly divorced sorrows. Knowing that nothing we see is ever *really* what we see—and that no one is ever (completely) happy—may have been the best reason for giving up that couch in the first place.

Driving away that evening while Josh napped, I began to picture a new-couch angel. He was wearing overalls in a cornfield, with grass stains on his knees and a white undershirt with holes in it; no idea why, but I've never been fond of the whole angels-in-white thing. He promised me I'd find something soon and smiled.

I smiled right back.

3
DAY OF ENDINGS

THE SUMMER WAS NEARLY half over by the time of *Tisha B'Av*. The ninth day of the month of *Av* is a time of endings, when Jews lament the destruction of both the First and Second Temples and other tragedies experienced by Jewish people throughout the centuries.

As the days in the synagogue home I had shared with my son Josh and his father were coming to a close, I had good reason to think of endings. Josh's dad and I had talked with our son about our separation and divorce. "This will always be your home," said his father, Mitch, "but your mom is going to a new home and I'm moving back here. Because we won't be married anymore, you'll be with your mom on some days every week in a new house, and other days here with me."

Josh had turned four in June, and though he was usually talkative, divorce had left him with little to say. His blue eyes were wide as he stared at his dad. He repeated the words, "This will always be your home," and said nothing more. I thought of Simone Weil's phrase about irreducible sadness, and how true that was for children who could not reduce the sorrow of their families breaking apart.

On Tisha B'Av, the *Book of Lamentations* is read, known as *Echa* for its first word, which is translated from the Hebrew as *Alas*. During Tisha B'Av, people fast and recite mourning prayers, and avoid washing, shaving, wearing cosmetics, and attending parties or celebrations.

Alas! Lonely sits the city
Once great with People! She that was great among nations
Is become like a widow;
The princess among states is become a thrall.
—*Lamentations, 1:1 Sefaria*

Two days after the Ninth of Av I packed my suitcases; it was the last night I would spend in the synagogue house. Josh was with his dad, and I lay awake in his room, tossing and turning. I liked the new neighborhood I'd found on the north side of town, and in the past few months I had also found new friends and possibilities. But it was still a time of endings, and I would be lying if I said I was not afraid.

I thought of a story I'd heard in Jerusalem about Rabbi Akiva visiting the city after the Second Temple was destroyed. Akiva said it was time to rejoice because the destruction of the Temple meant prophecies about Jewish people returning to Jerusalem would come true. Then I thought of the Jungian notion saying basically the same thing; when misfortune strikes, think of it as the beginning of something new and better. When you have good luck, beware.

I'd like to say this worked, but it didn't. I felt literally as though I had made the bed I was lying in and wanted more than anything to get out of it. I had tried like everyone tries, and failed in a marriage I'd hoped would last; but we can never go backwards. I sat up in bed, looking out the window at the large expanse of lawn, mottled here and there by streetlights and the moon.

"My eyes are spent with tears. My heart is in tumult."
—Lamentations: 2:11

It felt like a giant ghost was settling inside my chest and planned to stay for quite some time. I had visited a new synagogue briefly on the Eve of Tisha B'Av, but could not bring myself to sit; the words of Echa were playing too loudly in my head.

I started thinking instead about the Temples. *Were they really both destroyed the same day, or did the destruction happen in the same month? Were the days melded into one to commemorate both tragedies?* The two Temple buildings were distinctly different. The first was built by King Solomon and had been destroyed by the Babylonians. The famous song/saying, "If I forget thee O Jerusalem," may have been created during this time.

The Second Temple was built by Herod, and though he was hated, it was written in the Talmud that, "He who has not seen the Temple of Herod has never seen a beautiful building." Yet the Romans still destroyed it when the Jews resisted their rule.

I decided Akiva was wrong. There is no comfort in endings, no matter how much good might come to you at other times. We are creatures of the day, and we have only days (and nights) that must be lived through. Which doesn't mean you can't have hope.

The kindness of the Lord has not ended, His mercies are not spent.
They are renewed every morning—ample is Your grace!
"The Lord is my portion," I say with full heart; therefore will I
hope in Him.
—Lamentations: 21-23.

This was not what I had expected. But this was what I found; the lower floor of a duplex on a pretty street near a park; a part-time job with people I liked; and a New York theater called Circle Repertory, which had decided to produce a new play I had written about Jewish water rituals. Josh's dad and I had worked out a schedule that allowed Josh to see one of us almost every other day throughout the week.

Yet the heart cannot skip or laugh when it has lost something. The heart relies on the feet to walk slowly forward, on the hands to remake and recreate, on the eyes to look elsewhere, and the mouth to smile and speak when we don't feel like talking. Divorce, like death, forces us to reevaluate and then transform, and this too, perhaps, is the lesson of Tisha B'Av.

I opened the window, leaning out into the air. When I had told one of my friends about the divorce, she had said something that surprised me. "We are supposed to be fighters."

The Lamentations are repeated every summer, but when the day ends, we look to the New Year, with its new beginnings, to fly us full tilt into the light. No matter how many Temples have been destroyed, we are supposed to be fighters. And sometimes, that is all we have to carry us through.

4

ROSH HASHANAH RESTAURANT

YOU HEAR IT in synagogues by swaying congregations—whole swaths of people rising, like the moon. "On *Rosh Hashanah* it is written and on *Yom Kippur* it is sealed. Who shall live and who shall die . . ."

On Rosh Hashanah (the Jewish New Year), you don't use noisemakers or drink champagne. The start of Ten Days of Repentance lets you begin a new slate only if you're up for some serious soul-searching. The synagogues are packed and many attend only this time of year because Rosh Hashanah is designated as the time when our names are written in the *Book of Life* for the coming year. Or not. If you hope to change things, you must pray and ask forgiveness. The literal word for this process is *T'shuvah*, which means turning, as in turning yourself around.

Culturally, it is the opposite of our supposedly nonjudgmental culture. (Though if you've ever used social media, you know how judgmental we can be.) But the idea here is not to live and let live; it is instead to say who *will* live, who is living well, and who (maybe) will die.

The night Rosh Hashanah began, I was sitting in Muffuletta, a restaurant near the St. Paul campus of the University of Minnesota. I was not supposed to be there because it is *Yom Tov*, a holy day when one should not be at a restaurant where money is exchanged. I was with my new (and Catholic) friend John, who offered to be my "Rosh Hashanah *goy*" (non-Jew) and pay for the meal so I wouldn't have to open my purse during the holiday.

We had met in December the year before when I came to his house to interview an Arctic explorer for a play. John was one of the explorer's roommates, struggling with the breakup of a longtime relationship. Since I was struggling with the same thing, both of us held onto each other for dear life. When people asked if our relationship was romantic, I said it wasn't an attraction-type thing. It was a lot more like water in a drought, when friends were hard to come by.

As I picked up the menu I thought, *This is probably not going to get me into any Books of Life,* but John, who is a lawyer, said if anyone was judging I could try and explain the mitigating circumstances. I had been in Minnesota just a few years and most of the Jewish people I knew were congregants in my former husband's synagogue. I was divorced barely two months and didn't want to spend the evening staring at the walls while my son was with his father. So, Muffuletta's.

It may not have been the best way to observe the High Holy Days, but one cannot always choose the time of one's transformation. And in the last few months, I felt, I had transformed enough.

Salad? Yes. It wasn't terribly kosher to be in a restaurant, but I was still attempting to be. I tried to explain this to John, starting with the separation of dairy and meat, moving to the kinds of meat you could have and then separating meat and dairy dishes. A Jewish director had once told me, "Because God wanted us to be vegetarian, kosher laws were created to annoy you every time you wanted meat," I recalled.

I brought up the Book of Life and we discussed the afterlife. As a Catholic, John was puzzled by the Jews' approach, which seemed to be "there is, there isn't one," and left him completely confused. Wasn't the *Book of Life* proof there was some eternal One inviting people to heaven?

I always thought it meant your life extended another year, and you wouldn't die in horrific circumstances. But then, these Ten Days have always confused me too. I like the idea of starting over, mending one's life and relationships. On the other hand, the notion of punishing those who don't repent through illness or death leaves me with deep ambivalence about the judgment. If we see it as allegory, I said—

"What's the point?" John asked. "Why do any of it if it's only allegorical?"

"I don't know," I sighed.

John laughed, and we both said "Anyway" at the same time. I told him to go first.

"Well. There's a saying about how God paints in crooked lines," said John. "It's never a straight line. Not straightforward."

"I like that," I said.

We ordered vegetarian and I turned the forks and spoons over, trying to decide if we are really meant to be judging ourselves. If your marriage derailed, what part did you play in breaking it? If you're sitting in a restaurant instead of at the home of a Jewish friend, what can you do to make it count as a real Jewish holiday? Then my friend pulled something out of his satchel.

"Since it's New Year's," he said, "I thought you should have a present." I looked up in surprise. "We don't do gifts at New Year's—" I started to say. But he cut me off, saying something about his way of celebrating while handing me a present and an envelope. I opened the gift to find a framed photograph of me at his daughter's birthday party, both arms raised with a big smile.

"You look so happy here," John said, and I leaned forward to look at the picture, surprised to see my expression of joy—something I had not expected to feel, yet it was clearly present.

"Anyway, I thought you should have this," he said, looking at the envelope. When I opened it, I found a check made out to me for a hundred dollars.

"What's this?"

"Anne Frank," he replied, and I knew immediately what he meant. A few weeks before, John had written a column about Anne Frank for the *St. Paul Pioneer Press*. It was about how she could not be lumped in with other victims of other wars or even genocides, how one size does not fit all because we are all individuals whose stories are not transferable to other agendas.

At the time the column was written, newspapers paid on occasion to run them, so John received one hundred dollars for his work. He also knew when I moved out of my former home with Mitch, I left behind my first family sukkah. "I wanted to buy you a new sukkah for your brand-new life," he said. I had to bite my lip to stop the tears from filling my eyes.

So, Muffuletta. If you are ever divorced, and find yourself alone on Jewish New Year's, you do not have to go there. But if you do, you might find a fresh start between the garlic spread and salad, or the One who paints in crooked lines, leading us to the people we are supposed to meet. This One brought me a *sukkah* and a picture of me smiling; perhaps an early hint of future joys. And a High Holy Day I could write about—in a book of my own.

5

THE IMPORTANCE OF BEING EARNEST ON YOM KIPPUR

LIKE GWENDOLYN FAIRFAX in Oscar Wilde's *The Importance of Being Earnest*, I sometimes think Yom Kippur (the Day of Atonement) is a metaphysical holiday. When Gwendolyn's would-be suitor asks her if she would like him if he were not called Ernest, she refuses to answer. Instead, she says, "That is clearly a metaphysical speculation, and like most metaphysical speculations has very little reference at all to the actual facts of real life, as we know them."

To me, she sums up both the paradox and challenge of Yom Kippur. We are apologizing for a year of botches, missed opportunities, and cruelties petty and huge. We are trying to stay on God's good side, but we have seen too many examples of good people meeting horrific fates and deaths. So, what are we apologizing for? Does it really matter? And is there really a consequence or is it all, as the secular world would say, metaphysical speculation and mirrors?

On my first Yom Kippur as a single mother, I woke up grumpy, scowling, and snapping at my son when he wanted to play.

Being the mom of a four-year-old means you must make all the meals you usually do, but this time you cannot eat them. I served my son breakfast and we drove to my newly chosen synagogue, Beth Jacob. I brought my son to the babysitting room and stayed there a while, my mood lightening as I watched all the children. A tableful of snacks awaited them, and I had to leave before I reached for it.

I wasn't sure if God was listening, let alone loving and welcoming me back if I returned and repented. If I were good, say, truly good, and never cheated on things like *kashrut* (kosher laws) and observing *Shabbat* (the Sabbath), would I be more like Gwendolyn's Ernest—the perfect suitor? Or does God love me any old way and just want me to be better at being myself without the mistakes?

No idea.

On the way to the sanctuary, I looked out at the parking lot. A bumper sticker like the *No Whining* sign you see in offices says *No Lashon Hara,* meaning *no evil comments or gossip.* As a former cantor's wife who has been the subject of quite a lot of recent gossip, I couldn't help but feel a little better just looking at it.

If they were talking about me here, I couldn't hear them. I knew people at Mitch's synagogue were trying to come up with reasons for their cantor's divorce. Of course, no one wants to hear that breakups are never caused by just one thing, or that getting married young, which we had, can leave you unprepared for making a real marriage work. Instead of giving us some slack, the gossip surged fast and furious.

I had the feeling, though, that most of the congregants at my new synagogue didn't know much about my former life, and if they did, they weren't terribly interested. That was at least one thing, on this Yom Kippur morning, I was grateful for.

A few other things: most of the prayers were said in Hebrew, which is how I learned them, and though Beth Jacob services could be long, there was a lot more concentration on praying than I'd found anywhere else. Plus, the rabbi had a reputation for warmth and eloquence, and from the little I could see at this point, he was deserving of it.

There was also a soundproof room where people could hear prayers in the sanctuary while their babies or children were with them. The room had toys and a rocking chair and seemed like one of those simple-but-brilliant ideas rarely found in public buildings. I made a mental note to bring Josh there toward the end of the day.

Meanwhile, I took a seat at the back of the sanctuary and opened my prayer book to recite the liturgy. What interested me most about this was that, metaphysical or not, Yom Kippur was less about you than it was about your community. Whatever you may (or may not) have done, you were asked to make atonement as a group, not individually. The liturgy was not equivocal about the word *sin*, which included things like slander, lying, deceit in business dealings, passing judgment, running to do evil, and much more.

Even if you had not committed each and every sin, you apologized for them all because you don't want to embarrass someone who may be across the room. Or maybe you yourself didn't want to be embarrassed. The idea that we atoned not only for ourselves but for each other always struck me as something lovely—at the very least the opposite of pointing fingers at each other.

At the same time, the holiday asked us to take responsibility for ourselves—like me, for example. The process of separation and divorce made me anxious and grouchy around my child; there were many times I could have spoken more gently to him. Because we typically apologized to people we may have hurt, intentionally or not, on (or preferably before) Yom Kippur, I realized there was still something left I had to do before the end of the holiday.

The prayers continued as I left the sanctuary and opened the door of the babysitting room. I led my son out into the hall and could see almost immediately that he was ready to run outside. Instead, I brought him to the soundproof room overlooking the sanctuary. No one else was there and he quickly gravitated to a pop-up book left lying on the floor.

The rabbi was saying something about bowing to God, and

perhaps to those we may have wronged during the year. I told Josh I knew I hurt his feelings sometimes, including that morning. He stopped playing and looked at me with that secret ability children have to know when you are serious. I told him I was sorry that his father and I divorced, and I knew that had been hard for him. I said I had been grouchy and yelled when I shouldn't have and wanted to apologize. When I was finished, I bowed.

Then something happened that I did not expect. Josh bowed too, saying he was sorry for things he did that were wrong. "You know there weren't all that many," I said.

"Sometimes I yell too," he said. I smiled.

"Well, yeah, sometimes. I guess you do," I replied, thinking how lucky I was to have somehow gotten this old soul into my world.

And just then, in that moment, I caught a glimpse of my son's face that nearly sent me to the floor. His eyes held something I had not yet seen—not sadness exactly, but a recognition it was there and a kindness in meeting it. *Whatever our names are doesn't matter,* I thought, *because the day is giving us something.* A way to forgive each other and to make amends, so I know exactly what I'm apologizing for and Who (earnestly) is listening.

I took his hand.

6
SECRET HOLIDAY

FOR HAVING A HOUSE plunked right in the midst of it, *Sukkot* is a pretty secret holiday. It doesn't have the cachet of *Hanukkah*, which benefits from its showier neighbor Christmas, though Hanukkah is not nearly as important a holiday. Sukkot is unlike Passover, with its ritual *seder* dinner and eight days of bread-free complaining, and nowhere near as noticed as the Jewish New Year and Day of Atonement.

Yet Sukkot has its own mystique, a kind of covert charm tucked away inside a house large enough to fit at least eight people, with a roof that must be always only temporary and open to the sky. Sukkot is the Hebrew word for *booths,* and the holiday is so named because of the forty years Jews wandered in the desert after they fled out of Egypt. While there, they lived in booths, or make-shift dwellings, on the way to the Promised Land. Jews later made pilgrimages to the Holy Temple in Jerusalem, and erected booths on the way. Sukkot also commemorates the pilgrimages Jews made to Jerusalem in subsequent years.

The holiday is celebrated every fall, about five days after Yom

Kippur, but though I loved eating in the Sukkot at my Jewish elementary school, the truth is, I have seen very few Jews who celebrate it. Coming as it does at the end of the High Holy Days, Sukkot lives like a poor cousin in its little shack on the edge of a great plain of exhaustion, and is often left to rabbis, cantors, and synagogues so the rest of us can get on with our lives.

I must confess that I would not have celebrated it myself after leaving elementary school were it not for my marriage to a cantor; though we both started out as actors, my former husband was blessed with a rich baritone and a hunger for Jewish traditional music that brought us to St. Paul, Minnesota, and our first sukkah house.

These days, most Sukkot are built from prefabricated kits that are ordered from various firms around the country. Ours came from the local Lubavitch community, also known as observant Orthodox Jews or less kindly, black-hats. It contained several pine panels, plastic ties, and a slew of roof beams along with a deliberately cheery set of instructions.

The sukkah materials were delivered to our house, which sat across from my former husband's temple. I think being so close to the synagogue always made me feel like I was being watched. At the time, I remember thinking the sukkah gave me more privacy than the house itself.

The walls of the sukkah can be made of anything, as long as the booth has a minimum of three sides. Jewish families who do observe the holiday often decorate their sukkot quite elaborately, with Oriental carpets and wall hangings as well as vegetables and fruits that approximate the harvest. Sukkot is, in fact, a harvest holiday in addition to everything else it stands for, and most sukkot contain at least a few gourds and pumpkins, as well as their fair share of bees.

The roof beams of the sukkah are supposed to be augmented by evergreens, though finding them is something else again. It is worth noting that the roof should provide shade but allow air, sun, and stars to shine through so that we never forget the wanderers, and more importantly, the temporary aspect of our lives. We are here on borrowed time, whoever we are, and the holiday of Sukkot helps Jews to remember not their fragility, but the fragility of existence itself.

As a newly minted cantor's wife, I did not appreciate my sukkah. I was chafing in the role of a woman who wanted only to be immersed in theater and could not see the theater every sukkah provides.

There is a story by Isaac Bashevis Singer called *A Tale of Three Wishes* that occurs on *Hoshana Rabah*, the next-to-last night of Sukkot. I would not have known about it but for this story, in which the sky opens at midnight. According to Singer, this miraculous occurrence results in two children being granted three wishes, which end up, as in many stories of this kind, bringing them grief.

My own Sukkot story contained no miracles, nor even, directly speaking, any Jews beside myself. It was instead about a new friendship, the local paper, and—as mentioned in my chapter on the Jewish New Year—Anne Frank.

Somehow, she had captured the interest of my friend John, who had become my partner-in-crime for getting through the confusion of lost relationships. As often happens with people on perilous journeys, we talked endlessly and often, mostly about our trials, and how our different faiths helped us hold onto sanity, and ourselves.

John later told me he was exceptionally moved at a dinner I invited him to one evening to celebrate Shabbat (also known as *Shabbos*). Celebrated on Fridays and Saturdays, Shabbat began with lighting candles as we blessed and welcomed the weekly holiday. While watching me say the blessing, John recalled, he felt as though "the walls of your house blew away." He told me he saw centuries of Jewish women holding their hands over their eyes and praying.

I am not sure exactly if this was the reason John started thinking about Anne Frank, but we both thought it was great fun that the column he wrote about her ended up netting him one hundred dollars. If not for the Sukkot holiday, I think that would have been the end of it. What I came to realize when we were building it was that, like Christmas, holidays are best when they are seen through children's eyes.

The sukkah is put up for eight days every fall, and it is a sort of miracle that it stays up, given Minnesota's penchant for wintry weather in October. Because it is done only once a year, it is the kind of occasion children love—my son, no exception. I wanted that boy to have the same kind of excitement at my house that he would have when his father built the sukkah I left for him.

John hadn't ever seen my first sukkah, but I told him how I had purchased it from the Orthodox Lubavitchers, and how I had convened our neighbor's children, along with my son, to draw on its walls with sidewalk chalk so it would be properly decorated for the holiday. When John gave me the money I needed to buy a new sukkah, he also talked about new beginnings and saying yes to things. As he continued, I started thinking about my first Sukkot meal and how he and his children would be invited to it. Not very fancy, but exactly what this holiday meal should be—peanut butter sandwiches and apples.

We put it up on the side of my landlord's house in half an hour on a hot-bright autumn day two weeks later. John placed the beams of the roof so perfectly that I couldn't imagine ever being able to take the sukkah down. Unfortunately, the wind removed it the next day; we had to move the sukkah to the backyard where it was more protected.

Half a week later I sat in the sukkah after a biopsy that confirmed a lump in my breast was benign. I let the sunlight wash my face and shared a meal with my friend Sheila, deciding that perhaps miracles do happen after all. It's just that we don't know enough to recognize them. But if you look through the roof of a sukkah, you can almost always see the sky open.

It just depends on where you look, of course. And how far you are willing to go to be able to see your miracles.

7

THERE'S A STORY—I guess there's always a story about things like this—that says God brought the five books of Moses, called the *Torah,* to everyone else before it was accepted by the Jews.

"Will you take this?" God asked.

"What is in it?" they said.

"My commandments."

The Jews are supposed to have said, "All that God has commanded, we shall obey."

So, God shows up and asks if you want 613 laws. How to eat, when to cook, pray, do business, what holidays to observe, what to do when you wake up and what to put on the doorposts of your house. Of course, these are in addition to the basic ones, like do not steal, kill, or commit adultery. The laws on keeping kosher require books unto themselves, and there are thirty-nine activities forbidden on the Sabbath.

These are only a tiny portion of the laws. Yet the Jews bound all of them into two large scrolls that contain the five books. According to the story, they did not ask why. But if ancient Jewry was anything like my relatives, I'll never believe it. The Jews I know would never settle for anything without asking why.

Then there is another story. This one says if they didn't ask why, there could only be one reason. They were asking, "Why not?"

The Torah was given at Mount Sinai, after the Jews escaped Egypt and Pharaoh's armies. If God could free them so completely, they might have been thinking, how bad could his Torah be?

I pondered this in a synagogue, listening to a man playing accordion. It was *Simchat Torah*, the holiday when we celebrate the Torah and begin reading it each year. I had been on my own a few months and knew a few people slightly, but for the most part I was with strangers—being a very single stranger myself.

The accordionist played a medley of Klezmer tunes. There were children everywhere, and watching them, I missed my four-year-old. I had begun the dance most divorced parents know, giving their child up for one holiday and taking him for another. Watching the families around me, I could not help but wonder if it would always be that way.

The others began singing.

"Torah Simchat Lanu, Moshe!"

We sang, *"Torah brings us happiness, Moses."* But what did the law really bring, and why did so few Jews pay attention? Only a small number of the Jewish people I knew observed either Shabbat or kashrut. Yet there we were, dancing and singing in celebration of laws most of us barely adhered to, and that, at best, demanded a discipline we rarely have. I couldn't help wondering what everyone around me believed. I envied those who came to synagogue and drank deeply, because belief is never verbal. If you had it, I thought, it lived at a level many layers deeper than where thought begins.

When I was a child, I attended a Jewish day school and the celebrations of Simchat Torah were in the school cafeteria, with music, balloons, and caramel apples. The same caramel apples were in the synagogue here, arranged in shiny brown rows on a tray. I remember biting into the sticky-sweet side of the apple, the hard, sugary candy mixed with the tart skin of fruit breaking apart in my mouth, and how it came to symbolize the pleasure of the holiday.

I think scores of other children grew up thinking this way, too. I read somewhere that when Islamic children read the first words of the Koran, they are given honey so they'll think of something sweet when they read the words. Maybe caramel wrapped around the apples was supposed to be like the wrapping of the Torah, which unravels when we bite into it. But did treats and songs make it easier to observe?

In Orthodox neighborhoods, people were dancing in long lines, singing, laughing, and drinking wine. In a synagogue across town, my son was laughing, too. Then, someone next to me grabbed my hand and suddenly I was moving, the accordion music carrying me around the room, until I stopped caring about rules or restrictions. All I felt was the music. *Is that what Simchat Torah really was,* I thought?

As if in answer, Torah scrolls previously behind curtains around the room started appearing, and people dropped out of line to carry them. My son's father once told me a story about a poor village where they had no Torah. When the holiday came, they passed their babies around instead, raising them to the sky and kissing them. I thought of my son, dancing around with a miniature Torah at his father's synagogue. I could not help but smile at the thought.

Sweets and children, songs and laughter. We were celebrating joy, and the Torah was supposed to provide it.

Wait.

What?

The Torah I know never asked us to be happy. Instead, it demanded—honor parents, do unto others, give to those less fortunate, consider the repercussions of our appetites. It told us life is hard and we will want to escape it, to drown in food, drink, sex, drugs, shopping. It said there are limits, and to limit ourselves.

But it also told us to celebrate. To bless the moment, taste it, revel in it, sanctify it, see a baby as holy and raise it high, like a prayer. Most of us might not remember all the laws, but we can remember the sweetness. And in that sweetness, in the touch of someone's hand or the sound of an accordion, we might realize that even though we were divorced, or single, or lonely, we were not alone; we were part of a fabric, a story, and a tradition that carried us through the centuries to home.

So, if I was asked at this moment, "Would you take this Torah?" I would say at least, I'm glad someone took the laws—even if we were not able to keep them all.

Maybe, in a way, the rules made us more interesting, because even if we rejected them, we knew they are there, taking our measure. Maybe that's why we still dance around the Torah, because it stands, like a pillar, in the middle of all our messes and fears and dilemmas and happiness. And if we choose to, we can use it to see what we might be. Or become.

I mean, it's possible, right? Why not?

8

GETS, GOATS, AND MY JEWISH DIVORCE

IN THE WINTER before my first husband and I split up, I applied to the Jerome Foundation for a travel-study grant that involved going to the Canadian village Resolute. I was writing a play set in the Arctic and discovered Resolute through a conversation with Paul Schurke, who had been part of a North Pole expedition with explorers Will Steger and Ann Bancroft. Paul thought I would learn a lot by going to a place where winter stripped away all pretense of the civilized world.

I still have no idea how I would have pulled it off, exactly, as my son was only a toddler, but I believed his dad could be persuaded to manage on his own for the two or three weeks I was gone. In retrospect, I guess it was magical thinking, though if the grant had come through, I would have tried to carry out this last semi-marital adventure.

What attracted me most was the name *Resolute*. It seemed to connect directly to the next phase of my life, when I'd need the kind of strength people seemed to need in the Arctic. Instead of going there, I continued work on the play, met a few new friends (including another Arctic explorer), began to figure out the business of single parenting, and rolled, like a falling pebble, toward a secular and Jewish divorce. The more I found out about the Jewish divorce, though, the more I began to wish I'd run off to Resolute.

The divorce ceremony consisted of writing a decree and handing it to one's wife in front of a Jewish rabbinical court, known as a *bet din*. As I read through the words of the ceremony, it reminded me of the high priest who sent the scapegoat running into the wilderness in ancient Israel.

The divorce document, commonly known as a *get,* is also called a *Sefer k'ritut* (scroll of cutting off). It states the day, month, year, town, and other details, and then adds what movie people would call the money quote:

> I do release, send away, and put aside thee, my wife, . . . who hast been my wife from time past; and thus I do release thee, and send thee away and put thee aside, that thou mayest have permission and control over thyself to go to be married to any man that thou mayest desire; and no man shall hinder thee from this day forever, and thou art permitted to any man, and this shall be unto thee from me a bill of dismissal.

This *dismissal,* as mentioned, takes place in front of a rabbi, witnesses, and the scribe who writes the decree. Once the bet din is satisfied no one is coerced into divorce, the woman is told to remove any rings she has and to spread out her hands to receive the get. The husband places it in her hands, saying, "This is thy bill of divorce, and thou art divorced from me by it, and thou art permitted to any man."

When the husband is finished speaking, the wife closes her hands and lifts them up with the get in them. Then the rabbi takes it away from her, reads it a second time with the witnesses, and pronounces the ban of excommunication upon anyone who may attempt to invalidate it. Then he tears it crosswise, and as they say in cartoons, "That's all, folks."

As we came closer to the get ceremony, my misgivings blossomed into full-blown dread. I started thinking about ways to sabotage it—coming down with chicken pox or lying about a sick mother and going to visit her.

Instead, our synagogue's retired rabbi arranged it so the divorce was done with agents. "It's demeaning to the woman," he said. "I'll have it sent to you in the mail." It was interesting to me that even a rabbi felt this way, but in all the years the ceremony had been in existence, no one thought to change it. Why? And what would happen if more women attended? Would the ceremony change to reflect more equality between husband and wife?

It's said that even if you aren't a religious Jew, you should go through the *get* ceremony in case you marry another Jew and want your former marriage to be legally over, according to the Jewish faith. In other words, you're stuck for as long as Jewish divorces are required.

Thinking on it now, I believe my (almost) trip to the Arctic was an attempt to gain some sort of control over a time that made me feel scared and powerless. What I think I wanted, more than adventure, was acknowledgment from some Jewish source that getting a get doesn't mean you did something wrong, or that you yourself are wrong. Or if you did, the wrong was created by both of you as a couple—and neither one deserves to be dismissed.

Yet this archaic ceremony, like many Jewish ceremonies, remains unchanged year after year and century after century. I like that about most of them—but not about this one. Maybe it needs someone to open the windows to a Resolute wind that will blow away the smoke of ancient decrees and come up with something saner and kinder. Because divorcing people need kindness—wherever they are.

9

HANDS OF LIGHT: A TRAVELER'S HANUKKAH

IT SAT MUTELY on my shelf, a poor relation to the stone *menorah* (candelabrum), with its carvings of children holding up our candles every Hanukkah. THAT menorah was weighty with memories. THAT menorah stayed home.

I was packing for New York to see actors auditioning for my play at Circle Repertory Company. I was getting ready to stay with my friends Robert and Susan on West Seventy-First Street on the first night of Hanukkah, and though Robert was nominally Jewish, I was not at all sure they had a menorah.

I stared at the poor relation, with eight tiny sockets made of the flimsiest tin imaginable. In the center, a ninth socket was a bit taller than the rest; this would hold the *shammash* (servant) candle that lights all the other ones. Before I could talk myself out of it, I slipped the menorah into my suitcase.

It was my first Hanukkah as a single mom, though I wasn't parenting much that week. I was mainly a playwright in a city of playwrights, some Jewish, some not. My friends Susan and Robert were both agnostic, and while I hadn't decided on whether to celebrate the holiday, I didn't want to be menorahless if I could help it.

By the time I reached New York, I realized my friends might not have candles either. I rushed inside a store on Seventy-Second Street that was just about to close. There were boxes of "conventional" Hanukkah candles, each one a different color, and above those were tall, conical orange ones. I reached toward them and stopped; such grand lights for an ugly tin menorah. I reached for the conventional candles and paused again. "So?" the man behind the counter stared at me impatiently. "I'll take the regular size," I said, shoving them in my bag.

It was nearly dark by the time I rang the bell at Susan and Robert's, and as the foyer door opened, the scent of roast chicken mingled with the smell of other foods. There would be no potato *latkes* (pancakes) or songs; any Hanukkah here would have to be one of my own making. But what if I didn't make it? My son was with his father and stepmother and would have all the celebration he needed. And Hanukkah, with its chocolate coins and presents, seemed more a children's holiday than one for a newly single adult.

I climbed the stairs, frowning. I had a full three days of auditions and casting decisions ahead. I also had a vacation from my part-time job at home, and the burden of trying to recreate a Jewish life I wasn't even sure I wanted. So, it was Hanukkah. *So what?*

Susan hugged me and pulled off my coat while Robert nodded from his place at the piano. These two had been family to me ten years and better; Robert a musician and Susan an actor and dramaturge. Yet Robert and I had never talked about Jewish rituals, or anything else even remotely related to being a Jew. I knew his father had owned a delicatessen in Atlantic City, because he'd shown me how to slice a bagel once. I'd also heard Susan talking about the *bar mitzvahs* of Robert's cousins, and of course Robert knew my former spouse, since we'd all written a musical together before he became a cantor.

"We've got roast chicken and rhubarb pie," Susan said.

"You're the best," I replied, and she laughed.

As we ate, I thought about the menorah. *Would Robert mind if I brought it out?* I was never sure how he perceived me, or at least, the rituals he saw me observing these days.

When I was first getting separated, I spent a lot of wakeful nights, sometimes tossing and turning so much I thought I'd sail out of bed into the yard outside. While it was hard to fathom a future as a single mother economically and socially, the hardest thing was sleeping alone. Trying to imagine someone with me made it worse; but one night I hit on the idea of hands, with light streaming through their open fingers, blanketing me while I slept.

I called them the Hands of Light and became adept at using them to comfort myself when I lay down. The hands brought peace in ways few other things could; and if it wasn't faith, exactly, it felt close. But how do you explain that to someone who doesn't believe?

Of course, Robert wasn't looking for an explanation. And I didn't have one for him, really, only a vague feeling about light and luck and a poor man's menorah I'd carried for thousands of miles. A menorah that was waiting in my bag.

"Is it okay with you guys if we light Hanukkah candles?"

"Is it Hanukkah?" Robert asked.

I smiled and nodded.

"Sure," he said, shrugging. "I had no idea."

I pulled out the travel menorah, which was so fragile—chintzy, I should say—it nearly bent in two during the trip from Minnesota. I straightened it and set it on the table, where it caught the attention of Susan's cat, who jumped up and knocked it down.

"PHOEBE!" Susan yelled, pushing her cat off the table while I pulled the candles out. As I squeezed them into their sockets, I fantasized that lighting Hanukkah candles would bring luck to my new play. Susan handed me a book of matches; I struck one, lighting the shammash and sparking its flame.

I said the first blessing over the candles and then the second, trying to remember the melody as I thanked God for the oil that burned for eight days. Then came the third blessing thanking God for bringing us to this moment. As I sang, I saw Robert smiling, and the smile seemed to spread from his lips to his eyes.

Was I imagining this? Or was he thinking of his father's deli, of chocolate coins and *dreidel* games, played with a specially designed spinning top? I picked up the shammash and leaned it toward the lone candle standing on the menorah. It leapt into light and all three of us watched silently, as streetlights whitened the terraces outside.

The travel menorah was a lot like me, I thought. Bent over and needing to be straightened, I was sometimes lost at sea and sometimes lucky enough to be doing work I loved.

But wherever I go, there will always be part of me that needs this light, streaming out of candles and hands to say I'm stronger than I believe myself to be. What I do with it doesn't matter; it is enough to know I can find it, in a place too sacred to be shut or burned away.

10

WHAT DOESN'T KILL YOU

JANUARY. I WAS ON CLEVELAND AVENUE, a few miles north of the Jewish Community Center in St. Paul. I wasn't thinking about miracles, spring, or even the holiday called *Tu B'Shevat*. While I'd been in Minnesota seven years, I was still not used to driving on icy roads, and that day the ice was especially treacherous.

I was supposed to be at the Center in fifteen minutes for a Tu B'shevat meal, celebrating the day spring begins in Israel by eating Israeli nuts and fruits. I had volunteered to help serve the children in my son's class, and I didn't want to be late.

Like most moms with a working life, I was never quite on time when I should be, but I was still trying not to speed. Not that it was snowing—it had to warm up first—but since there was a lot of snow on the ground, the temperature had plunged below zero and made almost everything a solid sheet of white.

Yet we were celebrating the time when sap begins to run inside Israel's trees, as Jews have, apparently, for two thousand years, or at least since the Diaspora began. I was concentrating so hard on driving I barely registered the ambulance stopped at a corner, perpendicular to the intersection I was approaching. Was I supposed to slow down? Or was that just when they're alongside you?

Growing up in New York and New Jersey, I didn't have much cause to drive and only really learned how when I moved to the Midwest. I'd started out with a blue Nissan Sentra that I quickly fell in love with. But after Josh's dad and I divorced, I totaled the car on I-94 when the driver ahead of me jammed on her brakes.

At this point, I was driving a bright red Toyota, which had never felt quite right. It was much lighter than the Sentra and seemed prone to skidding no matter what I did. Because I bought the car during the summer, I had no inkling of how susceptible it was to winter winds and snow. The car was so light I jokingly called it Little Feather. And that's just how it felt when I stepped on the brake to avoid the ambulance.

Skidding.

Left, right, left again. Before I knew it, I was sailing up, up, up, over the curve and onto the lawn of a vanilla stucco house at breakneck speed. In less than a split second I was driving toward two trees, and it seemed very clear I was going to hit them. There was no time to think, scream, blink, anything. Just trees, coming toward my windshield. Trees whose sap was not running, though it would be in spring if I lived to see the sap run.

Hard, cold, gray, trunks, two or three feet around and coming toward me.

And then not.

Suddenly. Not.

I have no idea how I did it, but I skirted through both pillars, swerving like Steve McQueen in *Bullit* back down to the street, pointed in the same direction I had been when I started. Against all odds, there were no cars in front or behind me. And that ambulance, like a sleeping cat, was right where it was when my skidding began. Stopped, it seems, with no intention of moving.

I stared at the ambulance window, wondering if its driver was staring at me. In a minute or two, I thought, *you could have had quite the customer.* I started to laugh, then, turning from trees to ambulance to my hands on the wheel. I laughed so hard I nearly split my pants, then stopped and laughed some more.

And then it occurred to me—*thank you.* There is a prayer, I thought, you say when you have escaped danger. Something to do with a miracle, but I could not quite remember the words. *Baruch Atah*, Blessed are You . . . *HaShem melech olum,* King of the world . . . the ending wouldn't come. So, I finished in English instead. *Thank You for not being so busy getting the sap to run in Israel that You couldn't scoot me safely between two living trees.*

I waved at the ambulance and went on my way. God only knows what the driver was thinking. By the time I reached the Jewish Community Center, I was not only ready for Tu B'shevat, I was ready to celebrate. Figs, almonds, bokser fruit from the carob tree, and dates lined the tables. One of the parents serving with me was Orthodox and wore a skullcap and fringes (a.k.a. *kippah* and *tzitzit*). I told him what happened on the road and said it felt like a little miracle.

"Big miracle," he muttered, turning away to pour juice for the kids. I looked at my son, reaching for a date and popping it into his mouth. It was not just the sap that is running, I decided. It was our blood, eyes, and bones. It was the One who made us able to anticipate, apprehend, use our reflexes. It was the miracle of movement and humor and speech. And then I remembered the prayer. *Thank You, God, for making me a miracle . . . nase gadol ba z'man ha zeh.*

Some years later, my mother died, and I was barely able to cross the street without feeling like my heart had been wrenched out of my chest. Crumpling tissues in my rabbi's office, I asked him, finally, if he believed there was life after death. I thought he might mention God, but he spoke instead of sap. This mysterious, liquefied nourishment spread like wildfire every spring through plants and trees to tell us there might be something like a resurrection.

But maybe resurrection isn't limited to what happens after death. Maybe it can happen on the road to the JCC, to your office, or to a meal with a friend. Maybe somehow or other, for no reason, you can be saved and live to tell about it, even in January. To me, that will always be Tu B'Shevat.

———

11

DOES YOUR MOM COOK ON SHABBAT? A KID'S EYE VIEW

"DOES YOUR MOTHER COOK on Shabbat?"

"Do you turn the light on? Watch TV or play the radio?"

I was six years old, riding the bus home from Jewish day school. Barry and Norman, two boys in fourth grade who rode the bus with me, were preparing an inquisition. Normally they'd be fighting, pulling each other's ears back and pinching noses until one or the other screamed. But for some reason at this point, they had decided to focus on me.

"Yes," I said.

All hell broke loose.

I was not raised in a religious home, and my father hadn't been either. My mother's family may have kept up the Jewish dietary laws in Russia, but once they emigrated and my mom got married, her own mother told her not to worry if my father didn't want kosher food. We went to synagogue a few times a year, for High Holydays, Passover, select events, and bar mitzvahs. I knew that the meat we ate wasn't kosher, and I certainly remember a few cheeseburgers eaten in restaurants. I even remember a time my mother served something she referred to as "Virginia corned beef." It turned out to be ham.

I didn't much like it and never had much of a taste for ham or pork, but knowing my homelife was anything but exemplary according to my schoolmates made me feel torn and embarrassed for many years.

"If your mother cooks on Shabbat and you watch TV, you're not being Jewish," Barry said. "You're not being the kind of Jew HaShem wants you to be."

I stared at the boys, having no idea what to say. They had barely talked to me for most of the year, and I still have no idea why they decided to question me. Finally, I told them I didn't know the answer to their questions, and for some reason, that satisfied them, and they went back to torturing each other. Yet this episode has stayed with me, a reminder that I am still wrestling with my own notions of Shabbat and how I grew up.

When I got home that day, I tried to ask my mother why we weren't good Jews, and then to persuade her to observe Shabbat and keep kosher. She was, however, having none of it.

"God cares about whether or not you are a good person, not about whether you cook on Shabbos or eat special food."

"But why are you sending me to this school if you don't care about the Torah or Jewish laws?" I asked.

"Because it's a good school and you are getting a good education. End of story."

So, there we left it, or she did. I began to lead a double life, steeping myself in Jewish culture like a tea bag every morning and leaving it after school. At home, I left things that didn't seem kosher on my plate—or spit them out in a napkin when no one could see. On Shabbat, I said prayers in my room or tried to wheedle my mother into taking me to synagogue.

My dad worked every Saturday until four in the afternoon and slept most of Sunday, so I never expected he would go to services and didn't ask. Both parents said they were proud of the way I could speak Hebrew and we always celebrated Hanukkah, Passover, Rosh Hashanah, and Yom Kippur. Yet somehow, Shabbat and all its rules—along with lots of other rules and customs—were not on the radar.

When I left day school in seventh grade, I went to a public school where kids grew up in homes like my own, but it wasn't long before I started missing my old friends, who were funny and tough but who would never give a thought to how you looked or dressed. Though I didn't match their level of observance, I wasn't like the kids in my new school either. It often felt like I didn't really belong anywhere.

At the new school there was no talk of Shabbat, but everyone wanted to know what you were wearing to school dances on Friday night. It made me miss the stories of my first-grade teacher about families dressing in their best clothes on Shabbat and gathering for a special dinner. Though we had a lot of holidays, the teacher said, Shabbat was the biggest one of all.

Yet my family didn't celebrate.

By the time I went to college, I had largely forgotten about Shabbat, but years later, my actor husband decided to become a cantor and I confronted the holiday once more. Though there were a lot of rules and I sometimes struggled with them, I started to love the feeling I would get on Friday nights, one of celebration and peace.

When the marriage ended, I struggled to create a Shabbat that would bring me that same feeling. I tried it with friends, with my son and me by ourselves, on synagogue picnics, and at the homes of Orthodox families with elaborately paced rituals. I believe now I couldn't find it because what I wanted was to be celebrating in my own home, with a partner I loved romantically.

My best Shabbats began when I invited my new boyfriend over and lit candles for the holiday. By the time we got married two years later, we had shared some exceptional Shabbatot—with my son Josh and alone—and my husband had developed a taste for *challah*, the festive bread Jews eat on Shabbat, by candlelight.

Thinking back on my school bus days, I still remember my discomfort as a child in the presence of two holier-than-thou terrors on the day school bus. My Russian émigré grandparents fled a country that despised them as Jews; and their children likely absorbed the shame of their own parents' experience. Yet here were two religious children doling out shame to someone who they didn't think was Jewish enough.

Can we ever stop shaming each other?

If Shabbat is a day of rest, maybe it can also be a rest from judgment.

If I saw Barry and Norman now, I would tell them to stop asking me what my mother was doing on Shabbat and grow some manners. If my parents were here, I would ask them to come over for Shabbat and wear my best clothes to welcome them. Because the school I attended shed new light on our traditions, and now I know that. In their own way, my parents were trying to give me pride they never had—in being Jewish and lighting candles with those you love.

12
ONE-PARENT PURIM

OKAY, I KNOW YOU'RE OUT THERE—a freshly-made, unsuspecting single parent. You see other families celebrating Jewish holidays and look at your child, feeling like you have only half a family to give, and that half is mostly empty, like a hollowed-out log. Because observant Jewish families usually have two parents.

My first *Purim* holiday as a single mother happened with my friend John, who like me, was trying to stay afloat on the seas of single parenthood. Purim celebrates the ability of Jews to survive concerted attempts to destroy them—and is one of our most joyous holidays. To celebrate, I brought my son, Josh, to my friend's house with a box of three-sided pastries we call *hamantaschen*—and four finger puppets bought at a synagogue gift shop. I bought them because my son, like his mom before him, was a creative child, given to weaving stories with handkerchiefs, trucks, and imaginary friends.

The puppets were hardly masterpieces, with round button eyes that had roving dots in the center that often made them look cross-eyed. Queen Esther had curly blonde hair frizzing out horizontally, which couldn't have been remotely accurate. Her uncle Mordechai, the king and his evil vizier Haman looked so goofy I almost thought of using handkerchiefs instead but decided against it as I'd already paid for the puppets.

Josh had heard the *Megillah* scroll (Purim story) read at the synagogue where his father worked, but I knew he hadn't understood much, as the story is chanted in Hebrew. The story of Queen Esther, who married the Persian King Ahasuerus after he banished his former queen Vashti, and Esther's struggle to save the Jewish people would be lost on my four-year-old boy. So today was supposed to be about giving Josh and my friend's children a more child-friendly Purim story—if I could manage it.

The year before, I had been at synagogue with Josh and his dad, and before Josh was born, his father and I had been with a congregation in Indiana. My favorite Purim there was when the rabbi dressed in a white wedding gown, intoning passages from the Purim story in falsetto, and Josh's dad was dressed as Boy George. He and I had argued briefly over borrowing one of my favorite jackets, which had felt vaguely like an episode of *M*A*S*H* with a fight between Hot Lips and Klinger. But I did end up giving him the jacket, and he and the rabbi had made an entertaining comedy team.

The next year I had no synagogue to attend, as I hadn't yet joined another. I also hadn't the first idea how I was going to celebrate. I told John it was a Jewish holiday, but not much more. Now I stood in his kitchen listening to his three children play with my own, trying to figure out how to create a family Purim with what felt like a puppet family rather than a real one. Just a few months earlier, I had been part of a synagogue community where Josh's dad had explained the holidays. Now, I was on my own, without a trajectory someone else had defined—or an armature of structured support. So I did what I always do when I'm in trouble—tell a story.

I called out to my son. "Ready to share some of this hamantaschen?" Four pairs of feet scurried into the kitchen, and as I handed out the pastries, I started talking. "Once upon a time, there was a stupid king." I started that way because it was exactly what I heard my teacher say when I was in Hebrew day school and always thought it was a great way to begin.

"This king did whatever his advisers told him," I said, "and they wanted his wife, Vashti, to dance for him. She refused, so they banished her."

"How did that make the king stupid?" my friend's daughter Alison asked.

"He listened to his advisers without listening to his wife or caring about the consequences," I replied. "And then, the king became very lonely without his wife and realized he would need someone." I picked up the finger puppets to continue the story. "So. The king called for all the women in his kingdom to come to a gathering where he could choose a new wife. No one in the Jewish community wanted to go, because one of the king's advisors was a very evil man named Haman who wanted to kill the Jews."

"Why?" Alison asked again.

"He wanted people to bow down to him, and Jewish people would only bow when they were praying to God. So, Haman made it very hard for the Jews, plotting to make war on them. But a man named Mordechai convinced his niece to attend the gathering in hopes she might marry and gain the ear of the king."

The children's eyes were wide, intent, and fixed on the puppets as I moved them around the kitchen table. I explained how Esther tried to blend into the crowd, how the king was taken with her and selected her out of all the others, and how she grew close to him and eventually saved her people by telling him of Haman's plans.

I explained how hamantaschen are meant to symbolize Haman's hat and how we eat them as a symbol of victory. And by the time I finished telling the story, I realized I didn't need anyone else to give my son a piece of his heritage. Which was, in itself, a kind of victory.

I say this because—again—I know you're out there, and maybe this parenting business is new to you too and the thought of doing it alone is enough to send you screaming into the night. So, I wanted to share what Purim taught me that year; you don't need to depend on anyone else to teach your kids about the holidays. Whatever you do with them is fine—as long as you make them yours.

13

A HOLE IN THE FLOOR

I WAS IN LUND'S, an upscale grocery store which I am never in, because it costs more than I can usually pay. I was combing the shelves for the whole-wheat *matzah* (unleavened bread) I can't live without at Passover. I also needed dessert to bring to my hostess' Passover dinner celebration, which we call a seder. Whatever they had was not where it was last year.

Spying a smallish, older woman who appeared to be milling around the grape juice, I smiled hopefully. She returned the smile, and I took the plunge.

"Do you know where the Passover matzahs are?"

With a sweeping gesture, she indicated the aisle where everything was stored. They seemed to be expanding their stash of Passover goods, and that suited me fine.

Turned out the woman was from Russia. We ended up chatting for fifteen minutes between the chocolate seder plates and the Kedem grape juices. She asked me if I prepared for the holiday in the *traditional* way. I told her I did, though I wasn't raised in an Orthodox home.

In the early days of our marriage, my former spouse and I bought a few boxes of matzah, gave away our bread and pasta, and called it a day. When we moved to the Midwest and he became a cantor, we had to scrub countertops and cabinets and exchange dishes, pots, and everything else that came in contact with what the rabbis call *hametz*, or leavening. When a congregant said, "Passover is when you learn the meaning of slavery," I laughed. But I knew exactly what he meant.

Post-divorce, I had a choice. I could go back to my old ways, or, for consistency and my son's sake, I could wash, scrub, boil, change dishes, wash, scrub, and boil some more. With only two days to decide, I was still on the fence. Should I turn my house upside down to make sure we are really observing Passover, or could I get away with less? I looked at the Russian woman.

"I think I will probably start cleaning soon," I said, "though I'm not exactly sure why."

She told me the answer without knowing it. "My mother," she said, in her thick Russian accent, "used to bake her matzahs in secret, in the middle of the night, and stored them in a hole in our kitchen floor."

I could guess at the reason, but she told me anyway. "In Russia, we were not allowed to practice religion, and for Jews, it was extremely bad. My mother would never eat any bread during the holiday, but we—her children—ate it in school. She used to ask us to save some of the matzah, but what do children know? We ate most of it for supper. If she didn't have enough for the whole eight days, she went without. Now when I think of it, I want to cry."

She looked at me, as only tiny old ladies with crinkly blue eyes and Russian accents can. "Zo, my dear. Happy Passover. May you enjoy in good health."

We went on, she and I, to our separate ways, two days before the holiday. I knew that if I decided to continue the tradition, I would have to come home after working all day and start cleaning. My son would say he'd help, but more likely that wouldn't happen, and I'd be up very late scrubbing and grumbling to myself.

I knew that in two days my breaded days would be over. And my mouth started watering for the bread I wouldn't have. I was doing this, why? Because my mother, and her mother, and all the generations I can possibly imagine and can't imagine from centuries before, did it.

Because as a friend once said when I sat at his seder table, Jewish people have survived centuries of oppression, since no matter what they say or do to us, we keep our traditions.

Because eating matzah for eight days wasn't enough; I needed to clear the room, clear my head, clear a space for it.

Because when all is said and done, preparing the house for Passover gives me a new way to talk to God.

It doesn't involve prayer, which is traditionally how we are supposed to connect with God. It involves an action I can take, a taste, a change in the way I eat, drink, use my dishes. It says I am here, I am present, I am living the holiday in a very particular way and space and time. *I am listening to it*, and in doing so, giving God a way to listen to me, and to all of us, who are trying to be Jewish—in hiding or in the light.

Because when I sit down for the first seder, every single year since I've been a child, I get a feeling of being lifted up, and it stays with me all night, because Judaism is not so much about language or prayers or ideas as it is about the sanctification of small things, the things we do in our homes, when we are eating, getting ready for bed or work, and telling the stories of people we never met but who did the very same things we are doing. Because Passover encompasses all these things in a single week.

Because this Russian lady had to hide her matzah in a hole in the floor and her mother wouldn't eat if she ran out of it. And I can eat matzah in the office where I work, and my son Josh can eat it at school.

Because if Josh didn't have the experience of matzahs and seders, I would be guilty of a kind of child abuse.

Because of all these things, I will go and scrub and wipe and lift and haul and get ready for Passover.

And my heart, like the hearts of others might be when it is two days before Christmas or Easter, will be light. At least after the dishes are done. And the cabinets. And the stove.

14
THE BEGGAR IS WAITING

GROWING UP, we didn't talk about it at home. The *Shoah* (Holocaust) entered my life through a second-grade teacher in Jewish day school who began telling us the horrific memories she couldn't forget. When I shared these memories with my parents, they acknowledged that yes, they had happened, but didn't elaborate. At nine, I read Anne Frank's diary, and then a raft of movies and books on the subject seemed to be everywhere. As a Jewish child, I became completely immersed in them.

As an adult, there came a point where I stopped reading these books and seeing movies or plays. I could see them without reading them, feel them without knowing them. What concerns me more these days is not so much the Holocaust—terrible though it was— but the way we live now, and where the *it* left us.

For me, this leads to my older sister.

As a child, she experienced anti-Semitic taunts and cruelty from other kids in her neighborhood where she and my parents lived until she was five. The children tied my sister to a tree, calling her a dirty Jew and forcing her to eat dirt and rocks. She was not even four when this happened and can't tell the story now without crying. Listening, I want to cry too.

As a teenager, my sister went to social events at my parents' synagogue, but these weren't religious events, and she did not attend day school. Jewish prayers, songs, and stories did not capture her imagination or even curiosity—so it was no surprise when she married a Catholic man and celebrated Christmas instead of Hanukkah.

What was a little more surprising—at least for me—was the decision to baptize her daughter at age twelve. When most Jewish girls would celebrate their bat mitzvahs, my niece joined the Catholic faith. While my sister said she didn't believe in the baptism rite or even Catholicism, she was drawn to it through the love her daughter received in her husband's family and the family of her daughter's babysitter. Something else moved her too—the idea that it was a lot easier to live in the world if you weren't Jewish.

If I wanted to argue with her, I had *Yom HaShoah* (the Day of Holocaust Remembrance) to prove me wrong. There were innumerable other examples, including my sister's memories of being attacked as a child. Even memories of my son hearing anti-Semitic slurs when he wore a kippah to public school reminded me that for many people, Jewish customs and traditions are to be scorned. I also had my own experiences—including a New York morning on the subway when a man, noticing a Star of David around my neck, called me a "fucking Jew bitch" and "dirty money-grubbing Jew whore." I got up and left the car. I could go on and on, but all these stories just come back to the same thing; it is easier, or it can feel a lot easier, not to be or admit you are a Jew.

My sister's decision had no effect on my love for her or her child, and they both knew how much I adored my niece's Catholic father. What did affect me profoundly was the notion that we can throw off our heritage and disengage ourselves from it without looking back. People killed in the Holocaust thought this was possible too, protesting when the gestapo came after them. So much Holocaust literature is filled with people saying, "But we were so German! We celebrated Christmas! We were baptized!" And they were.

The philosopher Hannah Arendt, who grew up saturated in German culture before the Holocaust, was raised in a home where the word Jew was seldom mentioned. Are the brilliant books she wrote influenced by her prejudice against non-German or religious Jews? I believe they are. But was she given even the smallest amount of pride in being Jewish? Not by her parents or the times she lived in.

What about current times? Are they still essentially the same? If baptism could save my niece from a lifetime of pain and prejudice, why wasn't I applauding it? When my sister first told me her baptism plans, I couldn't help but wonder if some of the hatred transferred to us by other people has been internalized. The American melting pot, the changes of the 1960s and subsequent decades were supposed to make religion superfluous in some ways, to make the idea of *Jew* or *Christian* obsolete. The state of Israel was supposed to make Jewish people stronger, and for some, well, maybe it did.

But something keeps nagging at me.

We are still growing up excoriated, a lot or a little, for being Jews. It may not happen as often as it did to our parents; for some it may only occur occasionally, and if you're lucky, not at all. But the shame we feel when it does occur has somehow survived Israel, the Jewish-American revival in American schools and synagogues, the music, books, prayers, and rituals we have celebrated and recreated and *a lifetime of learning about the Holocaust*. What this means to me is that *something is still missing*; something we are ignoring, though as the poet Emma Lazarus once said, it is waiting for us like a beggar, waiting and hoping we'll turn around.

Emma said the beggar was God.

I cannot speak to the choices we make about religion, but I do not think we can ignore the rich and complex heritage Judaism has brought to us without losing a very crucial part of ourselves. And even if you kill us, that part will still survive.

On Yom HaShoah, we are called to remember the Holocaust, but I don't think it's enough anymore. We need to remember what we have as much as what we lost, how we observe Shabbat and speak Hebrew, and the very particular way we learned, in prayer and in synagogue, to speak to God. If we don't, we may still have the potential to be brilliant, like Hannah Arendt; but that brilliance will be hollow if all it is filled with is shame.

Whether it is easy to be a Jew may not really matter. It is what we discovered and what we've always known—before and after the Holocaust. We are here, we are Jewish, and we are who we are.

15

WHAT MY MOTHER DIDN'T TEACH ME

MOM. WHAT WERE YOU THINKING? You grew up in an Orthodox Jewish home, married a man who was not religious, so you were not observant, and then sent me to an Orthodox Jewish day school. And you know what? I loved it there.

It was called Yavneh Academy and I am happy to see it still exists. We prayed our *tefillot* (prayers) every morning, ate kosher lunches, and studied Hebrew for the same number of hours as English studies. When my friends Sari and Ofra invited me to dinner, I wanted to return the favor. But my mom called their mothers and explained that while she served kosher food, our dishes had not been separated—so dairy and meat were eaten on the same plates.

The result, of course, was that Sari and Ofra could not eat at my house. I was heartbroken and did not understand why my mother couldn't separate her dishes so my friends could be with us. The dishes did not change, and though my friends visited, their mothers picked them up well before dinner time.

As I grew older, I noticed that we kept kosher on holidays—other days, not so much. Yet, my mother often said she believed in God,

took me to *shul* (synagogue) now and again on Shabbat and insisted
we eat matzah on Passover. When I started talking about going out
on dates in high school, she refused to let me see anyone who wasn't
Jewish, and she wouldn't have tolerated it for a moment if I'd tried
to eat on Yom Kippur. But most of what I learned about observance
came from Yavneh—from the prayers, friends, Sukkot celebrations,
songs I learned in Hebrew and books I read, plays performed on
Purim—and the school's careful approach to food and kosher meals.

When I became a mother, I wanted consistency for my son. At
first, it was easy because his father was a cantor. When his father and
I divorced, I started with a cabinet full of meat dishes, an extra set of
silverware bought at Target, and a commitment to lighting candles
on Shabbat. Then came a second marriage to a non-Jew who said he
was okay with being kosher. He helped us build a sukkah and agreed
to a complete overhaul of every dish in the house during Passover.

But seeing how hard it was with only half our household
connected Jewishly often makes me think about my mom. She was
thrilled when Josh's dad became a cantor, though she hadn't really
been kosher since she left her own mother's house.

Would I describe her as a "twice a year Jew" who only went to
shul for the high holidays and the bar and bat mitzvahs of her friends'
children? She celebrated all the major holidays and was proud of her
family heritage and being Jewish. She made a mean hamantaschen
and a brisket you'd line up for in the cold. Other than that, well . . .
I don't know.

I think Judaism was my mother's childhood anchor and her home
team. She rooted for it and so did my dad—but, at least as long as I
knew them, they were never observant and didn't want to be. I can't
blame them because observance is hard. I've become convinced that
if you're going to follow the laws, you need support from a strong
community and friends. And even then it can be tough.

I'd have to say I've become less observant since my son graduated
from high school and went off to college. At the same time, I am glad

that whether my son was at my place or his father's, he celebrated Shabbat and had kosher food at home. He watched us light candles and build sukkot and searched the house for *chametz* (foods with leavening) before Passover. And if he wanted to bring an observant friend home, he could, since we had two sets of dishes and silverware.

My mother passed, and we never did talk about her approach to Jewish life. I think she was like most American Jews in the 1960s who wanted to hold on to pieces of the culture and assimilate at the same time. It was harder then to be different, and she wanted to fit in, be less like the girl she'd been in Borough Park, Brooklyn, and more like the girl next door. But why did she send me to an Orthodox day school?

I get that she thought it would offer me a higher level of education than other schools. But when I think about it now, though, I'm not so sure. There were other good private schools with good reputations. But Yavneh had something more—a bilingual, supportive Jewish atmosphere where being kosher meant you didn't have to eat alone.

Writing these stories now, I can't help but think of her. It's been a while since we could celebrate holidays together, but I remember the many things she gave me, knowingly or not. I think of Yavneh as a sort of secret gift. By sending me there, she helped create my earliest memories of Jewish holidays and prayers and an approach to living and language. I got the discipline I would need as an adult and as a writer. Most of all I got something to shoot for when I became a mother—a coherent approach to the religion we shared.

Am I saying Jewish day school is extremely important? Or that my mother could ease up on raising me Jewishly because the school did the rest? Yes . . . and maybe; I don't know. I *can* tell you my son decided to become a cantor, and I know his grandmother would be proud of him.

When I first heard of my son's plans, I wondered if that meant I needed to be more careful again about what's at my table, getting to shul and all the rules. *Mom? What would you say?*

16

ARE WE THERE YET? STANDING AT SINAI

WE WERE SITTING on the steps at the Jewish Community Center, watching SUVs pull in and out of the parking lot. They were weaving, swerving, cutting off people in smaller cars and scaring everyone else off the road. My friend Craig and I were waiting for our sons' childcare bus to return from a field trip. "Aren't they supposed to be more considerate here or something?" he asked. "At the JCC?"

I looked at the SUV drivers hunched over their wheels. "They look like goblins in there."

He squints. "Hard and dark."

"Like wolves."

Craig was in some kind of Christian or ecumenical seminary school, and that afternoon, he wanted to talk to me about God. Or about what it would be like if we stopped thinking there was a God.

"In class today I asked, 'What if there wasn't anyone up there? If we made it all up as a story?'"

"What did people think of that?" I asked.

"They all got quiet," Craig said. "But it was the first time, I think, that we were all being honest with each other. That we could actually think about what we were doing in seminary school—and in life."

"You say that because you're a playwright," I told him.

"What's that got to do with anything? So are you."

We sat in silence for a bit. "Do you believe Jews are chosen above all other people?" he finally asked.

"Chosen for what?" I replied. "Suffering?" He looked as though he wanted to kick me. I thought about asking him if they talked about Jewish holidays in the seminary like *Shavuot*, when Jewish people celebrate being chosen to receive the Torah at Mount Sinai. The holiday was approaching, but I decided against it. Shavuot is too obscure a holiday even for many Jews; it would be too much to think it would be noticed at my friend's seminary.

Hard, dark, wolfish was all around us. Not just the SUV drivers at the JCC, but a city and state and country full and neither the Torah nor the New Testament seemed to have made a lot of headway. People don't have time to worship God anymore—only celebrities. Yet on the coming Shavuot, I was planning to take my son, Josh, to synagogue. Of course, his father asked if I was going to, and I said yes. I never wanted Josh to think the only place he could be Jewish was at his father's synagogue.

The bus pulled into the parking lot and our boys spilled out with the other children, holding feathers and crayons. Craig and I said goodbye, and as I drove home, I thought about what he said.

Who is the story, God or us? There comes a time in every story, and especially in every play, when you must let go of your characters, let them do whatever it is they're going to do. They act and speak on their own, and all you are doing is moving them through. Is that what happens with us, and is God the ultimate playwright? I debated with myself about asking Craig this but didn't believe he'd agree.

The next day was warm, bright, and beautiful; we were on the cusp of summer. Shavuot feels new in ways other holidays can't approach. Like everything does in summer, it whispers a promise; *"I'll be gentle with you, I will be warm, and you won't have to fast or give up your leavening."* Even the name seems easy; Shavuot translates literally as *weeks,* which came after the Exodus and built up to the time Jews stood at the foot of the mountain to receive the Torah. And because we like to share each other's holidays, I invited my friend John.

We walked into the sanctuary, John and I, while Josh was in the children's babysitting room. Someone from the congregation was chanting a Torah trope, and as we edged closer to our seats, John looked at me. "Catholicism is old," he said. "But Judaism is ancient."

More chanting, and Hebrew prayers were sung and spoken. Because John was listening so intently, I heard them in a new way, hearing the ancient side of words I'd not thought about in ages. And I thought, *We may be hard, dark, and wolfish; and some of us even drive SUVs.* But all of us were standing at Sinai on this day, or at least that's what the rabbis said. And even if we didn't hear them, someone was chanting the Commandments—one to ten.

Do not steal. Do not kill. Do not covet. Honor mother and father. Love God . . .

I had a replica in my room when I was in grade school, black tablets etched on a white background. Black and white.

Bless the Sabbath and keep it holy. You shall have only one God. You shall not bear false witness.

Maybe instead of Jews being chosen, we did the choosing? As in, choosing to accept these laws. I don't know what my friend Craig would say about that, or even if it's true. But there is something here, in the letters, something ancient and eternal. Days and weeks full of holidays, and at this one, we stand together, holding each other up so we don't fall.

After the service we went outside, and I watched as Josh ran around the building with some of the other kids. Ever the gregarious Irishman, John started talking with someone while I turned to another friend. "We're not romantically involved," I said to her. "I hope people know that."

"I'll tell them," she said, and I laughed. If I had never been to this synagogue, it would still be familiar, and that is probably why I was here. I would know the prayers and the melodies, the syrupy taste of the *Kiddush* (sanctified) wine and the prayer shawls and kippahs. Does it matter what the day is or what we are celebrating? Or is the fact that we are here celebration enough?

If there were no laws and no Torah, there would not be this community, which fills something in me, though I couldn't name it if you asked. I *could* say it would feel right to be with them at Sinai. Maybe that would be enough.

17

"TELL ME A STORY about when I was a baby."

My son wanted to hear these stories all the time. I told him about how he loved to taste snow when we introduced him to winter, how he'd wail incessantly as an infant until we drove him to the airport, where the sound of planes taking off fascinated him. (I was sure he would become a flyer, but I was wrong.)

I didn't tell him this story, but I will tell it now.

My son was seven days old. I was holding him on my lap; he had just fallen asleep, and his tiny fingers unfurled like ribbons. He had no idea what was to happen tomorrow. No one talked about it; family members flew around me like birds as tears ran down my cheeks. Finally, my mother noticed.

"What's the matter, honey?"

I looked up at her. "*Brit* tomorrow."

Circumcision.

"That'll teach you to have a boy," my mother said.

Right, Mom. Thanks.

It was my fault, of course, marrying a cantor and having a

son. Now I was supposed to watch while someone, uh, cut his, uh, foreskin?

God. HaShem. We lost your name, but that's a whole other story.

Get me Rewrite, as producers say in old movies about Hollywood.

The cats stared at us with what I perceived to be sympathy. I told them (telepathically so no one heard) that I don't think there should be a party after the circumcision. Shouldn't it be private?

Across the room, everyone was laughing at a joke, but I couldn't hear it. If there were thoughts about the ceremony, no one was discussing them, and I didn't feel comfortable sharing mine.

Years ago, a friend told me that after her son's brit, she looked under his blanket. "Seeing this perfect little body with bandages. I hated that."

I was at that brit and from what I remember, some sort of topical anesthetic was used. I made a mental note to ask someone, remembering Josh's dad engaged a female pediatrician who doubled as a circumcisionist, known in the trade as a *mohel*. Funny word for an unfunny job. I thought of all the brit ceremonies I had gone to, never guessing at how a mother might feel until it was my turn.

I just got this beautiful, adorable, tiny little present, I thought. *We just named him. Joshua. I don't want to hurt him. I don't want to see him hurt.*

At this age, it's supposed to cause a minimum of pain and will never be remembered by the baby. At least that's what some people say, but they also say lobsters don't feel pain when they're being boiled to death. I wonder if the lobster knows better.

I looked down at my son again. What if we slipped away?

Two imaginary doors opened in my mind—one to a brit ritual with food, friends, family, and the other to me and my kid at the Greyhound Bus Station.

"Where you headed, miss?"

"California."

"Oh yeah?" said my imaginary bus driver. *"What's there?"*

"Renegade Jews who don't circumcise their children."

If there is such a group, wouldn't California be the place for them to be?

Maybe, like the cats, I could defy gravity and climb up to the ceiling with my son, hiding in plain sight until our demands were met. Wait a little longer, I'd say. Like until he's eighty or so?

Fantasies always end badly when you bump up against the *real*.

That night in bed, I listened to my son snoring in the bassinet. How did such a tiny nose make such big sounds?

I needed to talk to someone. But who? If there really is an afterlife, I would have asked for God's attorney. So many questions I wanted answered, and, I thought, *God will be too busy*. At this point I had some questions about the brit.

I could certainly wrap my mind around some of the other stuff. Shabbat, kashrut, even the ritual bath known as a *mikveh*. But this ritual, I just never understood. And there's no real explanation for it in Genesis that I could see.

And God said unto Abraham . . . ye shall be circumcised in the flesh of your foreskin; and it shall be a token of a covenant betwixt Me and you. And he that is eight days old shall be circumcised among you, every male throughout your generations. . . and the uncircumcised male who is not circumcised in the flesh of his foreskin, that shall be cut off from his people; he hath broken My covenant.

Got to give it to 'em for clarity, though.

In the *Guide for the Perplexed* (which would be me) the sage we call the Rambam says, "No one, however, should circumcise himself or his son for any other reason than pure faith."

So, although there is some scientific evidence about preventing cancer, urinary tract infections, and other illnesses, the tradition has always been focused on one thing and one thing only—God's commandment.

There are two kinds of people in the world. Those who believe, and those who do not. Which am I?

My son stopped snoring and I thought he was about to wake up. I looked over at him, but nothing happened.

Why did I think an attorney would help, anyway? Lawyers are so good at spinning things. This was a day when I needed the truth.

I couldn't refuse to do it, being in the middle of a cantor's family, and I'm not sure I could anyway, because God seemed to be so set on this. But why?

It felt to me like a symbol of everything I couldn't do, every possible way that I could not protect my son. Was that the point? Was it that he's Yours, and I'm only borrowing? If so, I get it. Don't need to prove it.

We don't need to do this now, I thought. *Do we?*

No reply.

The next day was bright and sunny. Josh's dad carried him out to the living room in a royal blue velvet shirt and pants. Everyone was cooing at him. When the doctor/mohel arrived, we talked a bit, and I received some reassurances. Some sort of numbing gel was applied, and the deed was done.

Suddenly, everyone was cheering and celebrating, but I couldn't wait to get my son back into his room. I've tried to remember little details but have blocked them out—whether Josh cried, how much gauze there was, and how long it stayed on.

I do remember leaving the guests and just sitting with my son for the rest of the day while he slept. I love so many of the things I celebrate Jewishly, light spiraling through candles, the Sukkot holiday, and *Tashlich*, the ceremony of forgiveness. But this one. I don't know.

I took a leap of faith for this brit. I took it because there are two kinds of people in the world, believers and those who don't believe. I still don't know which I am yet. But I think I know who I want to be—*mostly.*

Guess I have a ways to go.

MY SON WAS VERY YOUNG when I started thinking about the mikveh, the Jewish ritual bath used to ritually purify new converts and women about to get married and at the end of their menstrual cycle. The bath is mostly utilized now by Jews who are more observant, particularly in *Hasidic* (observant Orthodox) communities. Many feminists feel the idea behind it is that women's periods make us impure, and it is therefore a practice that should be discontinued.

My initial thoughts on going to the mikveh were similar. I didn't buy in to the idea that for three to seven days of every month, I was *niddah* (impure) because I was menstruating. Jewish marital laws call for women to wait until the end of the period and visit the bath before they can resume having sex with their husbands. Rabbis typically say men and women should stay away from each other during the five days of the period's average cycle, followed by seven days without bleeding, which adds up to about twelve. That usually means a woman is in her most fertile time, upping the chance she will get pregnant when she and her husband make love again.

Like many Jewish rituals, this one is chock full of rules, only in this case those rules are meant to govern the most intimate parts of a marriage. As it happened, Josh's father wasn't interested in this, and even if he was, I had a condition that meant my period would last between ten to twenty days every month, even though the bleeding was light. I went to doctor after doctor, and no one could help until I was sure I didn't want children anymore and could get surgery that stopped the period altogether. My prolonged periods didn't prevent me from having a child, but it certainly wasn't something that lent itself to the rules of the ritual bath.

The ritual itself is an interesting one. The individual wanting to participate in it must shower first and make sure he or she is completely clean so there is nothing to come between the person and the water. Jewelry, makeup, nail polish, fake nails, or even lotions are forbidden. In most Orthodox mikvehs, participants shower right at the mikveh center. An attendant then double checks to ensure that all possible barriers have been removed.

Once the attendant approves, the participant walks down seven steps into the mikveh bath, which symbolize the days it took for God to create the world. Participants immerse once, closing their eyes and crossing their arms over their stomachs to mark the difference between one's upper and lower body. At that point, a blessing is said.

Blessed are you, Eternal God, ruler of the universe, who sanctifies us through mitzvot and has enjoined us concerning immersion.

Women who are visiting the mikveh for marriage reasons immerse two more times, but converts and others, such as those recovering from a serious illness, say three blessings in all. Once the immersions are over, participants are free to go home and have sex with their partners.

A lot to unpack here, and I'm not sure I know where to start.

When I began thinking about this ritual, I knew many women

with no interest in going. I also knew my bleeding problems would prevent me from trying it, but the more I heard, the more intrigued I became. I can't exactly pinpoint the reasons why, but I can tell you my marriage seemed to be going south and our relations weren't exactly stellar.

At that point, the idea of holding off on sex for twelve days a month seemed like it might enliven the other days. I had heard that notion from Orthodox women I knew, and it seemed in some cases it happened.

When I spoke with friends about the marriage laws, many would wrinkle their noses and say, "No." But I don't believe playwrights have the right to say no, especially when it comes to venturing into parts unknown. And the more I heard about the mikveh, the more I wanted to write a play about it. I started my research by talking with the woman in my local community in charge of the ritual bath. I found her words fascinating and eloquent. She spoke of sexuality as something more than just getting physical, while acknowledging the importance of physical pleasure in our married lives. Rather than saying periods were impure, she said it was a time of ritual impurity—though I had a harder time with that.

I have been told that what ritual impurity really means is not being able to touch Torah scrolls or lead services. For me, that connects with the idea of women not being obligated to pray because they are taking care of children. In other words, mostly bunk—but that didn't mean I wanted to stop writing about the marriage laws.

The characters I started formulating were not even remotely observant. The husband was the chef at an Italian restaurant, and the wife owned a beauty salon. Neither regularly attended synagogue nor cared about being kosher. The wife's decision to go to the mikveh revolved around her wish to inject passion back into her marriage—and through a strange and circuitous process including the opposition of her mother and husband, she did.

My play, *A Body of Water*, became the second in a trilogy of one-acts about women and water rituals. While the play succeeded, my marriage did not. Of course, I don't think it was because I didn't attend the mikveh (she says with a grin).

On the other hand, I can't help but wonder if ritual baths help couples build anticipation over the course of long relationships. I think we tend to be creatures of novelty, and there are numerous books and magazine articles that say monogamy kills the excitement in a marriage.

But if you are a certain kind of person who likes to explore things, say, and your relationship is a good one, and you both agree, might the mikveh work for you? I heard thoughts like these from my friend Shoshanna, who may be using it still.

I can't tell you the answer personally, but that doesn't stop me from wondering about it. I still find it intriguing that women who are *not* observant are trying it. I will likely continue wondering—even if the only experiences I have are fictional ones.

19

NEW LIFE, OLD LIFE, NEW YEAR

WHAT HAPPENS TO US, ANYWAY? I told myself not to think about it.

It was a new year, getting close to the Jewish New Year Rosh Hashanah. I was in a hospital room with my mother who was dying of renal failure and in the end-stage of Alzheimer's. I marveled at my mother's eyes, deep and dark and set on high cheekbones. She looked so much like her brother. How did I miss that before?

We were in New Jersey and the hospital was understaffed, so everyone ignored us. I was trying to set things up so we could bring my mother home, but it was slow going. I had come straight to the hospital from the airport. Opening the door to my mother's room was like a descent into hell.

Instead of caring for my mother or trying to lessen her fear, she was left to her own devices. She had soiled herself and no one was changing her underclothes or hospital gown. Instead, they put her in restraints.

Mom had always been a force of nature—fierce, opinionated, with an artist's eye for strong composition—and she was always beautifully dressed. Seeing her whipping her head from side to side in fear and pain was a sight that still haunts me. If a nurse had been around at that moment, it would not have been pretty.

Luckily for staff on the floor, I had arrived with a nurse my sister and I hired to help us care for Mom once we got her home. Kathy ran her own home health agency, and though I had only talked with her on the phone before getting on the airplane, she had been an angel since we met.

As soon as we saw my mother, we untied the restraints. For a while, I could only cry and hold Mom's hand while Kathy wiped my mother's face and began feeding her Jell-O. When I told Kathy I was going to speak to the person in charge, she could tell I was going to scream at someone. She counseled me to be careful; in an understaffed place like this, the only thing we had on our side was getting the staff to like us.

I collected myself as best I could and greeted the head nurse. I told her my mother was not getting the care she needed, including new Depends and changing. I also made it clear we could not have restraints. The nurse dispatched an aide to my mother's room and said she would talk with staff about being more attentive. She also said restraints might be necessary if we weren't there, so I immediately resolved that my father and I would be present as much as possible until we could get my mother home.

When I had talked to Mom's doctor before leaving, she promised to visit within the next forty-eight hours. I assured her we would have care lined up at home so my mother could be discharged. I told Kathy I would do whatever it took to get Mom the homecare she needed along with the dignity and respect she deserved.

By the time we left, it was long after midnight. My mother was sleeping peacefully, and the night nurse said there would be no restraints on her watch. She told me I could call any time, and I took her up on it, at two and then five in the morning.

The next day, my father and I arrived mid-morning in a taxi, as

he was no longer able to drive and had recently sold his car. We tried
to get my mother to eat, smile, and talk to us. I washed her feet and
promised she would be home in a few days. My father looked out
the window, and I could tell he was trying not to cry. I glanced up at
the door, hoping something or someone would come in to save us,
and then saw a little girl.

She was tiny, maybe four years old, following her mother down
the hall. Her hair was curly and red, like mine at that age, and she
carried a basket of treats and New Year's cards. Her mother wore a
blue headscarf and a long dress and stockings. And suddenly, this
hospital, which I was cursing under my breath just a moment ago,
seemed a little less dark and forbidding.

"Happy New Year!" the little girl chirped. Her mother gave us a
card, and when I opened it, I found a number to call if you needed
rides to the hospital. I asked the woman about this, and she told me
to call her Shoshanna. If my father and I needed rides, she said, she
would be happy to help.

The girl's name was Rachel. She and her mother belonged to a
branch of Jewry we call *Hasidism*. The word comes from the Hebrew
word *hesed*, which means loving kindness. Hasidim are also called
"ultra-Orthodox" and other terms less flattering, depending on who
you talk to. For a long time, they were seen as outlaws in the Jewish
faith, at war with the established orthodoxy. Now, they represent
orthodoxy in an irony that would have given their founder, the *Baal
Shem Tov* (Master of the Good Name), a good laugh.

Rachel was growing up in a world rooted in the eighteenth
century. She will always wear long dresses and be likely to marry
young and then cover her hair with a scarf or wig. Her husband
and she will be part of a community that focuses most of its time
on observing the Torah commandments (*mitzvot*), which means all
613 of them.

Compared to Rachel's life, my own seems chaotic and haphazard.
My mother did not take me to visit the sick at Rachel's age—though

we did visit my gravely ill aunt, and I remember bringing her a honey cake for the New Year. But the home I grew up in would never be mistaken for Rachel's house. Watching Rachel and her mother at the hospital, I got hungry for the kind of childhood she had.

I knew I was romanticizing; I would probably chafe under all the restrictions Rachel lived with every day. But at that moment, with my mother's papery hand in mine, I longed for something solid and permanent, some way to find eternity in the life I saw disappearing before my eyes.

Mom had no idea Rosh Hashanah was coming, and I didn't even know if she would survive it. In fact, we talked on the phone just a few times after she went home from the hospital and I returned to Minnesota. I had planned to go back after the holidays, but she died before I could get there—so this week was all we would have.

When Mom's doctor arrived and worked through the logistics with us and the hospital social worker, we figured out that we could bring my mother home the next day, as long as Kathy's nurse was there. I called Kathy, who confirmed that was the case.

I hung up the phone and told my father what was happening. Rachel offered me a cookie, and I realized I hadn't eaten since breakfast. I asked if she wanted a piece and she nodded, but her mother said they had to be leaving soon. Rachel trotted off behind her mother, bringing cards and food baskets to other rooms around the floor. A few minutes later, Shoshanna asked if we wanted a ride home. It was close to five o'clock and my father was exhausted.

Shoshanna led my father and I out to her car and I rode in the back with Rachel. The sun shone her curls up like copper and she stared at me, wondering why I didn't wear a scarf like her mom. Was I married? I was, but I was not observing the rules of modesty. Of course, I was imagining all this; we hadn't said a word to each other. I smiled at Rachel, who looked at me solemnly.

I couldn't tell her about my mother, and I knew all she had seen was a frail old woman in a hard white bed. When I was Rachel's age, the safest place in the world was my mother's lap, and if it was New Year's, we would be surrounded by relatives. I looked out the window, trying to stop the memories. I started to imagine Rachel's life instead.

She may have had a lot of brothers and sisters; I had only one. She never tasted anything that isn't kosher and probably never will. On Rosh Hashanah, she would sit with her mother in synagogue (calling it shul) in a section specifically set aside for women and girls. She would not be obligated to say prayers as she grows up because women's roles are more focused on family—yet I think she will.

Rosh Hashanah begins the start of Ten Days of Awe, and each day, Rachel would learn, is an opportunity to look at who you are and where you are going, as well as where you have been. It is a gateway to how you are inscribed in the Book of Life for another year, and it asks you to make choices and changes about how you live and what you think about. It is a time that encourages us to ask questions, as I was asking when I looked into my mother's eyes.

What could I say that will make this day better? What are the things we will never be able to say to each other?

This Rosh Hashanah, I thought about Rachel, about how I wanted her life while I watched my mother leaving it. If it was up to me, Rachel would never know losses. She brought me so much brightness on a day that was so dark. She will probably never know how much she and her mother did for us, and all the others in that hospital. I will never forget them; I have never been able to thank them.

I guess that's what happens to us.

20

BEFORE THE NEXT YOM KIPPUR

YOM KIPPUR is only twenty-four hours, but for me it starts way before that. During the New Year, we observe the Tashlich forgiveness ceremony by taking a handful of breadcrumbs, which, symbolically, casts off sins we want to throw away. We say a special prayer and throw the breadcrumbs into the water, trying to let go of past regrets. A few days later, we try to apologize to people we hurt and ask them to forgive us so that we can arrive at synagogue on the Day of Atonement with a minimum of baggage.

Every Tashlich, I think about my high school friend Sasha. The first time I saw her we were both fourteen, walking into homeroom together. She wore a red leotard and had just the right amount of makeup and poise. After school, I saw her smoking a cigarette, crushing it lightly under a heel with a gesture I wanted to imitate, but couldn't. It was practiced and at the same time, effortless. She was the apex of everything cool.

I was a much more awkward fourteen—pale and freckled, trying hard to get used to my contact lenses. I had no boyfriends while Sasha had many, yet somehow, we became friends. Throughout high school, she was one of the only people I could talk to who actually listened to me. I don't know that she was very happy—her parents were divorced, and she sometimes drank and used drugs like meth—but she had an intensity and honesty I couldn't find anywhere else.

After graduation, I went to college while Sasha found a young man named Jerry and married him. I saw them when I was home on vacations, and they looked beautiful together, tossing jokes at each other and laughing. They had a little boy and an Irish setter and teased me about having the same color hair as their dog.

A few years later, I got married too, and my husband and I honeymooned at cottages owned by Jerry's parents in rural Maine. It was an idyllic holiday, and they didn't charge us a dime. Perhaps being up there, seeing the ocean and mountains and pines, made me think Sasha's life was idyllic too.

My mistake.

I can't remember when she started telling me the truth about what was happening at home. I just remember picking up the phone one day and going still, hearing words like "bruises" and "black and blue." While she was talking, I tried to picture Jerry, sunny-faced Jerry, throwing Sasha onto the floor and kicking her.

When she was pregnant with her second child, I visited to see what I could do. It was close to Christmas and the house was full of poinsettias. Sasha looked up at me listlessly and I remember being shocked at how dark the circles were under her eyes. She talked about the violence, but with a baby coming, she didn't feel ready to pick up and leave. And no matter what I said, she was adamant. She wasn't going anywhere.

After her son was born, things got worse, and Sasha began to call more frequently. It was not a time when there were many domestic shelters—though she wouldn't have gone even if there were. And the police seemed to be either unable or unwilling to help.

I tried to convince Sasha to leave the marriage, though I wasn't very good at it. I didn't understand why she couldn't just go to her dad's house, where I knew she would be welcomed. I didn't understand her pride, or wanting to make it work, or any number of reasons why she wouldn't quit her husband. I wanted to beat him myself, and I often felt helpless. After a while, when I saw that I couldn't change anything, I just got too frustrated and turned away.

Instead of picking up the phone when my friend called, I let the call go to voicemail. Sometimes I talked to her and told her things I wanted her to do. When she argued against them, I got upset and didn't want to talk any longer. After a while she stopped calling, and I didn't stay in touch.

When I moved to Minnesota I started thinking of her again, but by then it was too late; she had disappeared. I tried calling, but the number I had for Sasha was disconnected, and she didn't appear on any of the social media sites I checked.

Now she is everywhere and nowhere. Sometimes she wears a red leotard and is walking into a high school class. Sometimes I imagine her in the dark when I come home, with flat, dead eyes looking up at the ceiling. At Tashlich this year, I threw away all my breadcrumbs; but I know there is one that will stick to me—and unless I can find my friend, it always will.

On Yom Kippur, like everyone else in synagogue, I bring my own prayers and demons. I lay them on the floor of the sanctuary, looking down at my prayer book and intoning the words,

B'rosh Hashanah tik-a tay voon, B'yom tzom Kippur tik-a-tay moon. On Rosh Hashanah it is written; on Yom Kippur it is sealed.

I see the words and think, *This was not a mistake I made. It was more.*

For the sin which we have committed before You in passing judgment . . .

For the sin which we have committed before You by a confused heart.

My heart was confused and frightened. I couldn't figure out how to help my friend, so I abandoned her.

For all these, God of pardon, pardon us, forgive us, atone for us.

And God says, *Find her!* And I say, *I'd give anything to find her.* Before the next Yom Kippur.

21

SUKKAH DELICIOUS

THE NIGHT BEFORE I LEFT, they gave me a party and a brooch. In the center was a rhinestone circle inside a map of Brooklyn. "So you'll always know where you are," said my friend Jorie. I still have the brooch in my jewelry box.

When I left Brooklyn and moved to the Midwest, I couldn't find friends to match those I left behind. We weren't so much close as *tight*, swimming in a stream of artists in plays, nightclubs, and Renaissance fairs. Leaving opened a hole the size of a canyon inside me. I kept looking for what I had and eventually gave up on finding it.

Then suddenly one year at Sukkot, interesting things started to happen, including my friend John buying me a new sukkah. Other friends invited me to a sukkah party, and we turned on Middle Eastern music and belly danced. They invited me to seders and Shabbat dinners and book clubs, and we started, for want of a better word, to *see* each other. They could see me. I could see them.

On one Sukkot, my friends' party was in the evening. Inside everyone was smiling, bustling, cooking, stretching their fingers out for sneaky bites of chocolate, and yelling to be heard above the din.

The sukkah was on the porch, and though it was not traditional in the sense that you couldn't see the sky, the open windows brought in air and the gathering darkness.

The room was decorated with the bright, dry flowers of fall, and we sat on cushions on the floor. We lit candles and sat with our dishes in our laps; it grew darker as we ate and talked.

There is something to be said for eating delicious sukkah food in the dark next to people who know and care about you.

After dinner the talking grew softer, more intense. Some people left and the rest of us drew closer—our hosts Paul and Paula, their son and daughters, Aaron, Leora, and Nadia, with Leora's fiancé and Nadia's husband and their new baby, Maya. I was sitting across from Beth and Dianne, women I could easily talk to for hours. I have known everyone here for enough years to be able to know their faces in the dark and to recognize the rhythms of their voices, whether close or far away.

We talked about holidays, and Beth asked if we should get together once a month on Shabbat. It could be potluck so the host or hostess wouldn't have to cook, and we could make whatever we felt like. I started grinning, remembering dinners in New York with friends in younger days.

There is something about a circle of close friends that makes you taller, more beautiful, and stronger. You can be who you are, and all you have to do is walk in the door and fit like a puzzle piece into a world you own. There are no stairs to climb, no interviews, no auditions; you can plug in and light up the room or shrink to the corner and read a magazine. Whatever you do, you will be part of these people and they will be part of you, whenever you are together.

When I moved, I thought I'd lost that feeling forever. You get busy, you get married, and you get kids, or you get divorced and then work, work, work until there's no time for anyone. So you wait for Sukkot, which brings an island of peace in the fall before Thanksgiving descends with its more traditional family dinners. You take time to decorate the sukkah, remembering the booths built by ancient Israelite tribes on their way to Jerusalem to worship in the Holy of Holies.

Or you don't remember. You think instead of building the little booths now, nailing in boards and hanging branches of dried corn and willow. You make picnic foods and put on sweaters, and when your friend tells you she lost something precious in her life or that she is afraid, you listen, you give her that gift, because she is your friend. And you know you can also tell her you feel lost a lot too, and afraid that you won't get to where you always wanted to go before you die.

And then, without meaning to, you feel alive in ways you can't remember feeling for a very long time. There is nothing special, really, that you can point to, just sharing confidences and planning dinners, laughing at a baby's yawn, or hearing a friend tell you something they would never share with anyone else. But add it all up and the world is a little better, softer, and rounder, and your candles burn a bit hotter and brighter. You are home, and you don't need a brooch to tell you so.

Of course, my friends in New York are still very much part of me, and I see them whenever I can. I am grateful too for my family, and heaven knows they keep me alive more than anyone. But the power we gain in friendships is something else again. I've stood on stages and bowed to a roomful of applause; I've sung harmonies under tents with bandmates and thanked strangers for their kindness and praise. But nothing has made me stronger than my friends.

On the first night of Sukkot, we say a blessing said on other holidays too, thanking God for bringing us to this moment. As it happens, at this sukkah party, the plans we made for Shabbat didn't materialize as well as they should; we got busy and slacked off, and it would not be until Hanukkah that I see my friends again. But the memory of this evening in October is still blessing me. Like Sukkot, these friendships may be impermanent, fragile, and mortal—but no less lasting than the holidays they leave behind.

22

TREE HOUSE HANUKKAH

MY SON'S EYES were earnest and wide, repeating his father's words. "Santa doesn't really bring the presents. Parents do," he said.

"Right, Josh, but we can't tell those children because their parents want them to believe in Santa. And who really knows, anyway? We have beliefs too that may sound impossible to other people. We must respect their beliefs if we want them to respect ours."

We were in the airport, getting ready to fly to New Jersey. The end of Hanukkah dovetailed with Christmas Eve, and I was taking Josh to visit my sister because I had a week off and it seemed a good time to go.

My sister's husband was not Jewish, and she had been putting up a Christmas tree for many years. My son's father knew this, and I could feel his consternation in our son's eyes. Troubled eyes, and it fell to me to uncloud them.

"You know Aunt Les is married to someone who isn't Jewish, and they have a Christmas tree," I said. "But Aunt Les is still Jewish."

He looked at me. "You and my dad both said Jewish people don't have Christmas trees."

The surety of a five-year-old, as strong as granite. No bend or give in either the surface or the base. I needed to find a crack somewhere, to insert a little gray.

"Your aunt is sharing her husband's holiday," I said, "just like if we had a visitor who stopped by on Hanukkah and watched us light our menorah. And we're sharing a little of his holiday because we're visiting their home."

Josh seemed to accept this explanation for the moment. His dad and his dad's new wife have armed him well, telling him that Christian children got presents on Christmas for only one day. Meanwhile, Jewish children got eight days of presents at Hanukkah. They also got latkes and Hanukkah parties with grab bag games and dreidels.

I had no worries about my son being tempted by a tree or Santa Claus. Of course, that could all change once we arrived and he saw the tree with presents. But my gut was telling me it wouldn't phase him, which turned out to be right.

He enjoyed his uncle's banter, took a picture by the decorated tree, and even helped set up a plate of carrots and celery for Santa's reindeer. Then he asked me if we could light the menorah for the last night of Hanukkah, and we did.

His uncle was very enthusiastic when we brought out our traveling menorah and lit the candles. Aunt Lesley watched too with a silent smile and, knowing the roots of her disinterest in Jewish life, I decided that whatever happened during the weekend, I was not going to fret about it.

On the other hand, a new wrinkle had entered our lives, and I wasn't quite sure how Josh and I were going to navigate it. I had started seeing a man who was not Jewish, and though I had been trying to tell myself it wasn't serious, I could feel us both being pulled into something that was.

Josh liked my friend Pete, and both were connecting in ways I'd really wanted to see. I was not sure what we would do about Christmas if a relationship became permanent; would the idea of *sharing* someone's holiday work on a yearly basis?

Perhaps it was too soon to ask, let alone tell.

I called Pete after dinner and ended up talking to his mother, who had enormous warmth and a quicksilver wit. I could tell where Pete gets his sense of humor; she seemed like someone I would enjoy sitting down with, and I had a feeling she would be good at making me laugh.

Like him.

Hannukah, Christmas, Jewish New Year's, and Sukkot. *We'd likely weigh the balance of holidays down,* I thought, *because there are so many Jewish holidays.* Most Christians see only Hanukkah and have no idea of all the other days Jews observe.

Pete got on the phone, and it was easy, easy, easy to talk to him. It hadn't been this easy to talk to anyone in quite some time. Josh got on the phone and chattered away at him, too.

We hung up and I turned back to my sister's Christmas tree, but at that point, the menorah was in the corner of my eye, a splash of light in the corner of a frame.

Hanukkah versus Christmas. No winners.

I didn't ask, but wondered. How much of a holiday can you share?

23

ESTHER, ME, AND THE "I" WORD

WAS SHE CROUCHING? Her face emerged behind the shoulder of another woman, wrapped in a dark veil so no one would see her. This was Esther, trying as hard as she could to escape the eyes of the King, who saw her anyway. He could see only her eyes, but the brightness came through to him, made stronger by the fact that she wanted to hide it. Yet he saw, and it made him choose her above all others. This brightness was, I think, a love of learning—Esther wanting always to know more.

I was at a Purim celebration on Grand Avenue in St. Paul, thinking of Queen Esther's ancient story. When she first married the Persian King Ahasuerus, he did not know she was Jewish, and his vizier Haman was trying to eradicate the Jews in the kingdom where Esther lived. By the time the king discovered Esther's faith, he didn't care, having fallen in love with a spirit that could only have come from his queen's willingness to meet life head on.

Josh danced with other children and then settled in to watch a Purim play. My friend Melody sat next to me, having brought her daughter, who is Josh's age.

"I always feel bad on Jewish holidays," she said.

"What do you mean?" I asked.

"Because I didn't marry someone Jewish."

Of course, I thought. This is the story of our generation, the children of immigrants' children who married outside the Jewish faith. When I was growing up, it wasn't quite forbidden, but close. There were hushed conversations my mother had about this or that one who fell in love with a Catholic—in my youth, they were always Catholic—and the heartbreaking dilemma faced by the couple.

Some families ritually mourned over intermarried sons and daughters, as though they were dead. Others gossiped about couples of differing faiths, calling the non-Jewish women *shiksas.* But it would be unfair to say that Jewish misgivings about intermarriage were restricted to older generations. There can still be an atmosphere of discomfort for people who choose to *marry out,* as the saying goes. I found it in my former spouse's synagogue, where a congregant said Jews who marry Christians "are finishing what Hitler started" because they are destroying Judaism for future generations.

She gets no points for the Hitler analogy. But I believe she was struggling with how intermarriage can change a culture, and a couple's children can grow up knowing little or nothing of Judaism. Because our religion is matrilineal, Jewish women may have it easier in terms of whether their children are considered Jews in rabbinic law. For Jewish men, this is not the case, and some ask their brides to convert. I have to say, though, that doesn't always work out so well, either.

No matter how you slice it, intermarriage is still a prickly subject. While writers like Philip Roth penned some fascinating novels with the ideas I'm raising here, people in Orthodox and Conservative Jewish communities are still struggling with them.

It had been almost two years since I separated from Josh's father, about eight months since the divorce became final. Now, like my friend, I was seeing someone who wasn't Jewish, though it had not been my intention to get involved. In fact, I had tried hard not to, like Esther did centuries ago. Perhaps she and I had something in common.

Or did we? Esther married the Persian king at the request of her Uncle Mordecai, who hoped she would save her people from Haman's plot to destroy them. The Purim story ends with Esther's side winning and a great celebration for the Jews. But we never discover if she was able to introduce any Jewish customs into the king's family, or if her rituals were forbidden in his court.

In my case, Pete was extremely supportive of everything I did, including Jewish rituals. We had known each other a few years, but I had never thought of him as anything more than a friend. After Josh's dad and I broke up, Pete had pursued me, but slowly, knowing I wasn't ready for a relationship. I even told my sister we had nothing in common, but she cautioned me that values were more important than interests. "You can teach someone interests, but if you don't have the same values, there's nothing you can do," she said, suggesting I give the man a chance. She herself had long since given up on the idea of going out with Jewish men.

As time went by, things seemed to gel in ways I hadn't expected. One, Pete not only liked my son Josh, but he had a real rapport with him. Two, being with Pete didn't feel like work—it felt like home. I didn't want to admit that, necessarily, and had teased him early on to create some distance between us.

"You must have lots of ladies you can go out with," I had said.

"I'm looking for someone to stay in with," he replied, and I had to acknowledge I always admired a man who was good at turning a phrase.

Still, it took me a while before I invited Pete to celebrate Shabbat with us. But when I did, he brought flowers and even tried to sing some of the blessings. Subsequent Shabbats made us both more comfortable with the day and with each other. I didn't get the feeling that he would want to convert, but it seemed if I wanted a kosher home and Jewish celebrations, he would be right there with me. Was that enough?

I looked at Melody, who felt like an outsider because she had married out. Would that happen to me? Would I lose my community being with Pete? What would that mean for Josh? Should I continue seeing him or look harder for a Jewish man?

Problem was, I did not want to look for someone else. I knew my son would grow up Jewishly since his father and I were both committed to raising him that way. But if I married an Episcopalian—even a nonobservant one—would it be easier for Josh to marry outside the faith too? And would that mean his children would grow up with Christmas trees as well as menorahs?

Did Esther have dilemmas like this too? Not that her story, with its heroism and sacrifices, had anything to do with my choices. But if Esther married a Persian king to make sure the Jews survived, doesn't Purim show us no one can break your faith if you believe in it strongly enough?

I looked around at the costumed children and turned to Melody. "You know, Esther wasn't married to a Jewish man, either. But she did all right, don't you think?" Melody looked at me, eyes widening, and then laughed.

"I'd be glad to celebrate with you any time," I said, and she took my hand.

"You've got a deal."

Fast forward here, not a lot, but a little bit. Turns out my feelings for Pete were stronger than tradition. So, reader, I married him.

Today, we are still together, and my son still identifies himself as a Jew, Christmas, Hanukkah, or otherwise. And every year during this time, I think of Esther. The lessons she learned might have been different if she married a Jewish man, but maybe—I don't know—she shone more brightly because life took her elsewhere. At least, I hope so—for us both.

24
ALL-FOR-ONE SEDER

SEDER FOR ALL, the words on the flyer proclaimed, like a rallying cry for Jewish Musketeers. Seder for all, or seder for none, because if you can't find a seder to go to, you'll end up at a seder for one.

At Passover time, Jews around the world begin the eight-day holiday with a ritual meal in a designated order (called seder in Hebrew), to remember our tribe's escape from slavery. Also known as the bread of our affliction, matzah makes its first appearance at this rite.

In most countries, there is a first-night seder and then another on the second night. That's because in ancient times, the rabbis (who are always decreeing something) decreed Passover and other Jewish holidays should be celebrated for two days by Jews who are dispersed throughout the world, outside of Israel. If you *are* in Israel, you celebrate most holidays for *one* night.

I know, I *know*; I don't understand it either, but the rabbis' explanation is so unhelpful it makes my head spin and yours would too, if I kept going there. The good thing about second-night seders is they are often more relaxed and less formal.

All over the city, country, state, Jews who are single by choice or necessity scramble to find a place at someone's table for seder one and seder two. Synagogues try to help by mailing flyers or sending emails asking congregants to invite people who may be alone. But if you are going to someone's seder because they've been asked to invite you, you cannot be wanted very much. Cannot feel wanted.

So, there are just times you do not go.

Do Christians feel this way on Easter? Don't even get me started on Thanksgiving. But this was *me*, two weeks before Passover, scouring madly through my address book in a last-ditch attempt to find friends I could either beg for a seder invitation, or, as a last resort, invite to a small seder of my own. I say small because I get a rash and run a fever at the thought of cooking for more than six people.

Since becoming a single mother and then a remarried mother with a non-Jewish spouse, I have scrambled, scrubbed, and done everything but defy gravity to get myself to Passover seders, whether others' or my own. Some years I lucked out with friends who happened to think of me; others I invited friends who were grateful not to have to make their own. Other years I called a good friend and begged an invitation.

When I was growing up in New Jersey, I never had to worry about such things. I was either at home or at my uncle Irving's, who performed the entire seder in Hebrew without cracking a smile. My mother's homemade horseradish was the hit of the evening and especially of my cousin Stewie, who I had a crush on. Once the seder ended, my cousins and I imbibed everything we could, from bad Passover wine to matzah ball soup, brisket, and *kugel* (noodle casserole) until we absorbed the holiday on the deepest and most cellular level.

Those days are long gone. After I moved to Minnesota, my son's father and I found many seder invitations through his congregation, but once the marriage went kaput, my invitations dried up too. I discovered that Jewish Minnesotans can be a notoriously close-knit community, and that finding a seder to attend was something on the order of scoring an invite to one of Andy Warhol's famous parties; you had to know someone—and know them WELL—to even think about getting in.

In my first year after divorcing, the week before Passover found me completely at sea. It was late, and I was trying to figure out if I should make a small second-night seder with my son Josh and invite our non-Jewish landlords so at least there would be someone with us at the table. The thought of this made me want to cry, so instead I indulged in a fantasy about Rocco Landesman, who is not only Jewish, but a famous Broadway producer. In my fantasy, I was related to Rocco (somehow). We lived in some Park Avenue townhouse and people would twist themselves every which way to be invited to our seders.

I imagined opening the door to welcome my guests, after watching dozens of winged Jewish pixies clean, scour, and *dehametz* the kitchen. (Yes, I know that's not a word, and no, I don't care.) I saw myself smiling, hugging, bringing coats to one of the bedrooms, pouring wine, reading the *Haggadah* (Exodus story), and trading insights with my guests. And I vowed to myself I would never, ever turn down a lonely singlet who wants to come to my seder.

But this townhouse lady was *not* me, and it was almost Passover.

Fortunately, I did wind up at seders with friends, and nearly every year since. I have figured out a way to bring friends to my table or to find a place at theirs. One year I was with a dear friend who was also going through a divorce; it was not long after 9/11 and it was just the two of us, as both our sons were with their dads on first-seder night. While it might seem a little spare to some, I had one of the best seders ever because it felt like a night for girlfriends. We read from the Haggadah, talked about past holidays and the state of the world, and shared a few secrets.

Other years I spent second-night seders with a couple and their numerous family members, and these were also some of my favorite times. The host, an amateur magician, created Houdini-like tricks to liven the evening, and his wife found ways for all of us to add poems, stories, and songs that made the seder our own.

Another favorite friend used toys and stories to make the seders memorable. Another welcomed everyone to one of the coolest lofts I've seen in the city, making us feel like we were in a Soho gallery surrounded by her paintings. One year, I was lucky enough to be in synagogue when a friend invited me to share her first-night table. I wanted to fall on my knees in gratitude right then and there. Still, I know I can't get lucky every year, and there may be Passovers without first- or second-night seders on my horizon. But that's okay.

The Park Avenue Rocco Landesman fantasy hasn't left me, and I suspect it will surface every Passover. What I like best about it is that I never have to worry about a seder invitation or prepping or cleaning up. Best of all, I have an imaginary family that never fights or scrambles or worries and that lives the Passover ideal to the fullest with exceptional desserts and clever stories.

Or maybe I've finally outgrown my Rocco. The friends whose tables I shared, or who have shared mine on occasion, are funny, clever, and creative. Our seder conversations are warm, thoughtful, even fascinating. And they're not relatives—so we have no reason to fight.

At the same time, I still know a lot of people out there who are still looking for seders. I think one day, I'll invite all of you to my house for a Passover seder. I'll take your coats, pour some wine, and we'll sit down together. I promise not to ask how you got here, but I'll listen if you tell me. And we'll know, without having to say so, that it's an evening that finally belongs to us. Seder for all, seder for one.

ON THE OTHER SIDE OF THE HOLOCAUST

THERE IS A POINT in Tony Kushner's play *Angels in America* when a flaming *alef*, the first letter of the Hebrew alphabet, flies across the stage. The alef is seen only by a character who is very sick with AIDS. As hallucinations go, this would have to be one of my favorites; if I was ever going mad, I believe the only thing that might possibly bring me back could be the letters of the Hebrew alphabet.

The letters were also prominent in the prayer books at the Great Synagogue in Jerusalem, when I stood at the doorway with a man who told me his parents had been victims of the Holocaust. The man said standing in the shul gave him "a certain satisfaction."

As far as I know, I did not lose relatives during the Holocaust. Both sets of my grandparents had landed at Ellis Island in the latter part of the nineteenth century; other relatives moved to Haifa from Italy, and from what I can tell, most everyone was either in America or Israel by the time the genocide started.

Like most Jewish children and adults, I have seen some of the most unbearable images captured during the Shoah through media images. I have watched people in Rwanda, Darfur, and Yugoslavia, among others, become victims of horrific genocides as well. I have never been able to shake the misery their stories left behind. My strongest reaction, though, is always anger; it doesn't even get close to sorry or sad. My anger can find no outlet, as the people perpetrating atrocities are not in my sights and I can't get rid of them. So, the anger stays coiled inside me, fermenting with nowhere to vent.

While I loved sharing the stories behind almost every other holiday, talking about the Holocaust with my son was next to impossible. I may have passed the buck, since I knew Josh would hear about it in school as I had. My parents never mentioned it to me until I came home after hearing one of my teachers share her story.

Some things, perhaps, can be shared by almost anyone but a parent and a child. Whether it was fear or overprotectiveness, I can't really say, but I think my anger had grown so large that I couldn't figure out how to communicate it in ways a young child would understand.

When I did think of talking about it with my son, I thought of the picture I had seen in a book of a boy, about seven or eight, with his hands upraised while, presumably, Nazi soldiers are pointing guns at him. He is pale, thin, staring at something just beyond the camera's range with eyes that seem as though they have long been defeated by darkness. I think of flying at the soldiers with a knife, knowing at the same time I would likely have been shot as well.

I don't want Josh to see this picture, even now. When he was a young child, I didn't want him to see any pictures of anyone being terrorized or slaughtered, or to ask me what they mean. I had no choice in this, knowing sooner or later he would see something and ask me, *why?* I always thought I wouldn't have an answer. I thought anything I said could never really explain the darkness that shadows our people like a plague.

I decided early on in my son's childhood that I needed something more on the other side of the Shoah, some way to bring the light back into his eyes after he heard about the six million, but where to begin?

While the media, books, films, and plays tell numerous stories about this time, there are barely any about Shabbat or other Jewish subjects or holidays. At least it seems so in comparison to what we see with the Shoah, which I still don't understand. Because if there's one way to fight back, at least from the vantage point we have now, wouldn't it be through those flaming alefs flying around like arrows onstage?

The Nazis did their best to destroy all evidence of Jewish culture, yet it trickled out. Anne Frank's diary, Hebrew prayer books, Shabbat candelabra, ceremonial objects, customs, foods, plays, films, and stories. These are the things I most wanted to give to my son, reciting the alphabet in the car as we sang it together when he began Hebrew school, sending him little notes in Hebrew with his lunch, lighting candles on Friday evening, and teaching him the blessings of the Shabbat-concluding ritual *Havdallah* as he reached up to smell the ritual spice.

Our books, our prayers, our songs and dances, language, music, holidays.

I wanted my son to remember our holidays.

Not just the big ones like New Year's and Hanukkah and Passover, but the lesser known as well—Shavuot and Sukkot and Tu B'Shvat. I wanted him to see flaming Hebrew letters lighting the sky above us when he dreamed at night, to bite into a fig inside a Sukkah before he went to school in the morning. I could not remotely even think about saving our people, but I can maybe save a little morsel of who we are and what we have now, and he could save it too. It may not be a lot, but it is something, and right now, it is all I have.

So instead of long discussions about the Holocaust, I took him out to Cecil's Deli and bought some Challah bread for the weekend. I made sure to teach him the blessings we said as we lit the candles to welcome Shabbat. I took this road because I hoped the memories of Jewish rituals we created—along with our love—would be more eternal and would not disappear into ashes, no matter what happens. The Hebrew alphabet that we call the *alef-bet* will bring us back.

"HE'S A LONG DRINK-OF-WATER man washed ashore in his thirties, marooned by the breakup of a relationship and drifting like tumbleweed."

So begins my journal entry during the first year of single parenthood.

"We met a few days before the New Year in December, both struggling with the same demons."

The next few months found us meeting whenever possible—sharing secrets, cookies, birthday parties, and field trips to each other's church and synagogue. Shavuot was John's first trip to my synagogue, Beth Jacob. I've shared a bit about that visit in a previous chapter, but wanted to flesh it out a bit more.

The first thing John saw was the rack of *tallises* (prayer shawls) and *kippot* outside the door. He asked if he should wear them, and I said it was up to him. He put on the kippah but not the tallis, which seemed right, especially as he'd never tried to wear one before.

We opened the door to the sanctuary, and as we neared our seats, we heard words from the Torah being chanted, which seemed exactly right, since the Torah was at the heart of this holiday. In fact, Shavuot always made me think of a waiting crowd at the foot of a mountain. They were waiting for something that would change their lives, but had no idea what it was or how it would reach them. You could almost say that's what John and I were going through in trying to recreate our lives.

The Torah brought Jews a set of laws that framed almost every aspect of living. I don't know how it affected the original tribes, but I don't know anyone now—unless maybe a rabbi—who observes all 613 laws. I do have friends who observe the holidays and think the net effect of these observances is to create a world outside of time. I'd have to say that's what I like best about them—riding on a wave that brings you to higher ground, where the realities of the world seem distant and small.

I think calling the holiday *Weeks* shows its core meaning is planted deeply in time. The Torah says it is a mitzvah to count the *Omer*, or the fifty days leading to Shavuot after Passover, to commemorate the offerings made in ancient times. Counting the Omer is a way to prepare for the Shavuot holiday and to remember how those at Sinai readied themselves to receive Torah.

There is no way, of course, to be ready for most anything. On this particular Shavuot holiday, I was missing my New York friends and the feeling of safety I had at my former spouse's synagogue. All around us were Jewish families, praying, chanting, or laughing together outside in the hall. All around us, time wedged itself up against the holiday and stretched out, waiting for the day to end.

Ahead for me: plays, novels, a new marriage, job changes, a growing son, a new house, the sorrow of watching my parents grow ill and die. Ahead for John: a growing business, a lengthy custody battle, a new direction in politics, and a popular blog read avidly on both sides of the aisle. He will also lose his mother and sister to cancer, and see his youngest son win a full scholarship to a music conservatory.

Ahead for both of us: 9/11, wars in Afghanistan, Iraq, and a new level of suicide bombings in Israel. There will also be new presidents, more and more polarization between parties, and endless conversations about the existence of God.

"Look at your hands," John said to me one night when I was sobbing, "I think we may really be alone down here." He told me to look at each thumb and finger, at my eyelashes and the color of my hair. "Look how cool they are," he said. "Who else could do that but God?"

All this was ahead, as we stood in the sanctuary on my first Shavuot as a single mom. The hours could only be measured by the chanting of Torah and the knowledge that it will outlast everything we know and dream, as generations count down the days to Shavuot.

After the service, John and I stopped by the children's room and brought Josh outside. The sun was so strong it was hard to keep my eyes open without sunglasses. I picked up Josh's tiny baseball cap and adjusted it to fit my own head. Both Josh and I were amazed I was able to perform this little magic trick. I decided it wouldn't happen except on Shavuot.

The night before, congregants had gathered as they do all over the world on the evening before Shavuot. The tradition is to stay up all night with a group of friends, munching dairy snacks and studying Torah. Why dairy? Some say it's to remember the stories of *milk and honey* waiting in the Promised Land, and others say dairy foods were typically produced during spring festivals like Shavuot.

Knowing people had been up all night studying and celebrating had a profound effect on me. I thought it yet another way of defying time. It also spoke volumes about what I was craving: a community, comfort, longstanding friendships, and a shared heritage. At this point, with a young son and a new job, staying up wasn't possible, but I told myself there would come a day when I could live this ritual and participate.

For the moment, though, there were an abundance of snacks

on the lawn, my son running through the grass playing with other kids, and my Catholic friend, allowing me to see and apprehend my heritage with new eyes. "Lot of beauty here," he said.

Timeless beauty—bringing both of us to higher ground.

27

INDIGO GIRLS AND INTERMARRIAGE: A MAGIC CARPET TALE

WE SAT ON THE RUG in the middle of the floor, and I told him we were on a magic carpet ride. Like Aladdin, I said, we were going up, up, up, over the city, and once we were high enough, my son could say anything he wanted, and it would be okay. I promised not to get upset at anything he said. We closed our eyes and pretended we were flying, and we were both very good at pretending. And then my five-year-old looked at me and said exactly what he wanted to say.

"I want you to get married, Mom."

His father and I had been divorced almost two years and his father had remarried. My son loved his stepmother and enjoyed spending time with her. I realized he may have thought our little home too quiet; or maybe he just wanted a more traditional family at our place too. I created these magic carpet times so he could tell me whatever's on his mind, and then he did.

"I want to get married too, Josh," I said. "But we have to be careful. We can't just marry anyone. We have to pick the right person. We're a package deal, you and me, and we go together. So, whoever we marry has to love both of us."

Josh looked at me nodding, and I could only hope he understood. Some days later, we were in the car, and he sighed. "I want you to get married, Mommy," he said. "But we have to be careful. We have to pick the right person. We can't just marry anyone."

I didn't know whether to laugh or cry. But it felt good to know, at least, that he was listening to me. And, though I wasn't ready to say so, I had most likely found someone, and that someone was Pete. He was not a Jewish man, but he was a wonderful man. I believed he would be fine if we invited him into our Jewish home, and though he wasn't kosher, he *was* vegetarian. Which is almost the same thing . . . right?

If you were to ask me why I made the decision to marry him, I could say a lot of things. I was impressed by his gentleness, humor, his genuine love for Josh, and his patience with both of us. Mainly, though, my decision was not rationally driven. It came about because of the Indigo Girls. Pete knew I liked them, and when we first started seeing each other, he asked me to go to a concert they were giving at the University of Minnesota. We got there only to find the concert was sold out. At that point, I decided the universe was trying to tell me that I should not be with this man.

I turned away from the box office just as a dark-haired woman entered the ticket booth. She looked directly at Pete, and I remember thinking, *She likes him.* Only instead of flirting, she asked if we were trying to see the Indigo Girls. "Yes, and you're all sold out," I said impatiently. And then, in what must be the start of some movie script somewhere, the woman smiled impishly and motioned us to come closer. That night, Pete and I had front row seats at the Indigo Girls.

So much for the universe.

One year later, Pete proposed, and I said yes. But I still had one more hurdle and no idea how to clear it. How do you create a wedding ceremony without a rabbi that honors your heritage when you're not getting married to a Jew?

The wedding was planned for the middle of the Sukkot holiday, with a civil judge officiating. I knew we would have no Hebrew and no ceremonial crunching of a wine glass underfoot, like most Jewish marriages. But I wanted Josh and everyone else to know we would keep our traditions, and that Pete was going to be part of them too. I talked to the judge about the holiday, and she said she'd think about it and get back to me.

On the morning of our wedding, Pete and I faced each other on the balcony of the University Club in St. Paul. The judge compared our marriage to a sukkah.

"It is not permanent, but it is the promise of a home," she said.

"Its openness pledges that there will be no secrets. The sukkah does not promise that love or hope or pledges will keep out weather or catastrophe, but its lines are a sketch for what might be. You have come together to celebrate your future together, the making of a home. We are reminded that the only thing that is real about a home is the people in it, who love and choose to be together, to be a family. So may it be for you now."

After the ceremony, we celebrated with Challah and said the *Motzi* blessing for bread. And though it was not by any stretch a Jewish wedding, I think the imagery of the sukkah has stayed with us throughout the years we've been together. I think Josh would also tell you he was raised Jewishly, in a Jewish home.

What this means for you and whatever weddings you may encounter, I don't know. I'm not recommending you do what I did. In fact, I think it's easier for Jews to marry other Jews because we are a minority culture in a not-always-hospitable world. But I do believe it's possible to bring your traditions with you wherever you go and to live them. And if you can manage to pick the right person, the universe has a way of responding—putting you up front and center with life—and maybe even the Indigo Girls.

28
CROOKED LINES

THE NINTH OF AV swoops in quickly, coloring the sky green and laced with blood like a tornado. Full of debris, it forces us to stop what we are doing and mourn. The First and Second Temples and the loss of parents, homes, children, lives.

While I was getting ready for my wedding and a new chance at love, my fiancé often told me, smiling, that Jews have too many holidays. I told him Tisha B'Av is my least favorite. Yet it seemed to me sometimes that we needed more than a day to mourn—and not just for ourselves.

Some years later, as we approached the day, I counted what had been a summer of losses. My best friend in high school collapsed some hours after a doctor's visit and died. He had a wife and daughter, and when we reconnected on Facebook, he told me how happy he was to have found them and everything else in his life. He had been a professor of literature and published eloquent, lyrical books about baseball and his favorite team—the Mets.

When we had been in high school together, my friend loved to tell stories, jumping around the room and gesturing wildly in a joyful, energetic dance. In our high school play, we were husband and wife in a production of *Look Homeward Angel*. One night I forgot some of my lines and he whispered them to me while lying on a couch amid a dramatic argument. We traveled to Europe together during sophomore year in college when I was nursing a broken heart. Though I was mostly a train wreck, I could not have asked for a better or more understanding friend.

Now gone. A few weeks later, a colleague from the Playwrights' Center was struck by a car after seeing a show in Minneapolis. He fell into a coma and died in less than two weeks—a gallant, funny, talented writer, and father of two daughters. His wife was my agent when I was doing voice-over work, and here I was reading her story on CaringBridge about her husband's last days. Not even a week later, a young man who was on my son's high school football team drowned while swimming with friends.

I open the *Book of Lamentations*, read every year on Tisha B'Av. I am drawn to the words inside and simultaneously repelled by them.

How doth the city sit solitary, that was full of people! How is she become as a widow!

Is it nothing to you, all ye that pass by? Behold, and see if there be any sorrow like unto my sorrow, which is done unto me, wherewith the Lord hath afflicted me in the day of his fierce anger. From above hath he sent fire into my bones, and it prevaileth against them: he hath spread a net for my feet, he hath turned me back: he hath made me desolate and faint all the day.

The words are, of course, a passionate rendition of suffering, which at the same time lays the suffering squarely at God's door while elevating the sorrow of the writer above all others. Yet even he must have seen that suffering was not only his lot. Did he think or even imagine the Temple would be rebuilt someday, or that human suffering would end?

Tisha B'Av is a fasting day, in remembrance of the destructions in 586 BCE by the Babylonians and in 70 CE by the Romans. The fasting—of course the hardest part of the holiday—is to remember the starvation of all the innocents in Jerusalem after the Temples were destroyed. It makes me think of infants in wars all over the world, staring out of news photographs with heartbreaking eyes. The words in Lamentations talk of suffering as punishment from an angry God. Reading that makes me angry, too.

I cannot believe that God is punishing people in the most heinous and diabolical ways for things we may have done, or not done. And if it is random, and God stands by while all this suffering continues, then what is the point? What are we praying for? Or to?

On Tisha B'Av we recognize death is all around us, that no matter who we are and where we live, it will find us, randomly and without regard for us as individuals, families, people, or tribes. As I write this, I'm seeing a 1930s movie star, someone snarly like Bette Davis, saying "God has nothing to do with it," in the middle of a party somewhere. How would she have written the book of Lamentations? I see her laughing when I ask. All of it has always been written. The words are carved into our souls.

I look down at the book and close it. I know what it is telling me; I do not need the words. It says life is bumpy, it has no shame. Yet we cling to it, and if God can really see us, I don't want to think of Him/Her as meting out cruelty because we haven't said enough prayers. I want instead to see God in the healing moments—in friends that reach out to us, in crooked lines that lead us to better places. Ever since John mentioned this when life was smacking both of us, I have never forgotten it.

The book says when the Temples were destroyed, the people were left desolate. Yet centuries later, our books and traditions are still here. Perhaps there is something good about being such a "stiff-necked people," as Biblical sources call us. Destruction may be imminent, but we are still, God help us, dreamers. And if you can dream a life, you can at least use those dreams to live it boldly so when the suffering comes, you can reach beyond it. Knowing it will pass? Or knowing you've done things that matter—or (okay, maybe) tried.

Every year, as the fasting day arrives, I pray Death will leave us alone for a while, knowing I cannot play him. But I hope he will take his time, at least, before reaching out his hand to us again. I open the Book of Lamentations and see no comfort in it. But if others are reading this book in synagogues around the country, I hope we will be here for each other when death and suffering land. Is that where God lives? On Tisha B'Av, it is what I am praying for.

29
FIRST HOUSE

IT WAS NOT LONG after I married him, and it was raining, hard enough to wet our faces as we bent over boards and beams. My new husband's full name was Peter Bullard Budd, though I've never actually called him that.

Inexplicably, we were both in good moods, or at least not complaining. I am not sure why except that being raised in a family of nonobservant Episcopalians probably means you don't whine. I tried to imitate him with limited success, being from a family of entrenched and inveterate *kvetchers* (complainers).

It was not only raining; it was starting to get dark. Because of me, Pete was out in our yard messing with a sukkah. While this one was given to me by my friend John, it quickly became a tradition for my new family—Pete, me, and my son, Josh, now Pete's stepson.

This is how you know someone loves you, I thought, *when he forgoes sitting inside by the fireplace you don't have and ventures out into the damp to build a shack (oops! booth!) for a holiday he's never heard of.* We had got far enough so two walls had been raised. I looked up at them, realizing we were about to run into a tree and would have to move everything backwards. Looking up made me think of the *lulav* branch and citron that we call an *etrog*. I realized I had never explained them to Pete.

In his family, traditions are more relaxed: Fourth of July at his family cabin, Christmas and New Year's, Thanksgiving. I, on the other hand, grew up with all sorts of Jewish holidays and none of them seemed even remotely relaxing. When I had been married to a cantor, observing holy days and rituals was commonplace. But after a couple of years on my own, and then remarried to someone who wasn't Jewish, I was starting over again.

How do you explain something like the lulav and etrog, let alone a sukkah? The first ones I ever saw were at my Jewish day-school in Patterson, New Jersey. I was six and had just begun to learn Hebrew. The teacher brought us into a large, bright sukkah decorated with paper chains and flowers. We sat at long tables covered with white tablecloths and ate chips and other snacks on paper plates. My teacher then brought out a lulav and etrog, which appeared to be something like a long willow branch and a fragrant lemon. But not exactly.

If you look in the Torah, you'll see there is a commandment in Leviticus to gather four species of tree branches:

On the first day you shall take the product of hadar trees, branches of palm trees, boughs of leafy trees, and willows of the brook, and you shall rejoice before HaShem your God seven days.

A lulav is a palm branch held together with two willow branches and three myrtle branches. During Sukkot, you are supposed to wave the lulav around and say special blessings. At the same time, you are holding the etrog. I've seen worshipers doing this on holidays and it has always made me smile. In fact, it can be quite funny to see people who always look well-dressed shaking these branches like disco dancers.

But thinking about lulav rituals also made me think of past holidays, which I didn't want to do. I looked at Pete instead. The boards were sliding around so much he decided to fetch a hammer and nails. The instructions said this would be the easiest construction job we would ever have, but I think they meant that for people who actually build things, which in any case would not be either one of us.

The rain seemed to subside a bit, but the wind picked up, and I was thinking about calling it quits and finishing later. At that moment, our next-door neighbor Katie came out with two steaming cups of coffee.

"I saw you guys out here and thought you could use this," she said. Katie wasn't Jewish and she had no idea what we were doing. But just the fact that us knocking around back here in this weather was enough to bring her out with warm drinks made the night less damp and cold. Maybe the sukkah had already brought three people together that otherwise might not be.

Or.

That could just be my look-on-the-bright-side attitude—though I'm not known for them, I promise. We pulled the walls back from the tree and raised a beam, me holding it up while Pete tied and nailed it into place. The roof would be made of these beams tied over with branches, though at that second even hundreds of branches didn't seem like they'd protect us much.

I know the sukkah was created to remind us of the migrants and pilgrims we were in deserts and forests throughout history. What it made me think of that night is that we can take nothing for granted, whether it's our marriages, relationships, bodies, or livelihoods.

Sukkot was created, I think, to give us the kind of joy and silliness we can find only in moments, knowing on the other side of rain are memories you nail together inch by inch with the taste of coffee on your tongue.

I didn't say this to Pete and didn't tell him about the lulav and etrog either. One can only do so much in the rain and putting up this sukkah was enough. Since we were renting our home, our little booth was actually the first house we had owned. Was that a sign of something? Impermanence, or not taking each other for granted? I preferred the latter. I believe he did, too.

30

A LETTER FOR MY NERVES

HALFWAY TO THE HOLIDAY, I started feeling nervous.

"Where is Josh going for Simchat Torah?" asked Josh's father.

"I don't know."

"Well, he should be somewhere, don't you think? Either with me or you. He's a Jewish kid and it's a Jewish holiday."

"You."

"Okay."

"Me."

"What?"

"You."

I sent Josh to his dad, knowing that if my son wasn't with me on Simchat Torah, I might not go to synagogue, or to the celebrations the night before.

Making me nervous was the Torah itself—and my new marriage. Or was it my old one? There may be zillions of intermarried couples, but I didn't know many who were formerly part of a family that included a Jewish clergy member. And trying to give my son a strong Jewish identity, as I promised to do both in marriage and divorce, was a promise I wanted to keep.

Two days before Simchat Torah, I investigated some of the things the Torah says about intermarriage:

"You shall not intermarry with them; you shall not give your daughter to his son, and you shall not take his daughter for your son." *Deuteronomy, 7:3.*

In Prophets, I read, "And that we shall not give our daughters to the peoples of the land, and we shall not take their daughters for our sons." *Nehemiah, 10:31.*

In Jewish Law, it is written, "The Torah forbids a Jew to enter a marital relationship with a non-Jew; be it a Jewish man to a non-Jewish woman, or a Jewish woman to a non-Jewish man." *Maimonides' Laws of Forbidden Relationships, 12:1.*

Reading this made me think of a conversation I overheard at the age of twelve between my mother and a friend. They were lamenting the fact that someone's daughter had fallen in love with someone who wasn't Jewish. The couple had encountered so much resistance from their families and religious communities, they had to break things off. This seemed to me the most devastating thing you could do to someone, but it was obviously, at least in my family, a very hard-and-fast rule.

This Maimonides. Was he ever in love? And what did he think about Moses, who married a non-Jewish woman, and Miriam his sister who was stricken with leprosy for telling others she disapproved? What about Esther and her Persian King, or Abraham and Hagar? How do we square their lives with traditional, unequivocal Torah law? Are some animals more equal than others, as George Orwell would say? Are these edicts a course in Hypocrisy 101? Because that's awfully what they seem to be.

While the rabbi at my synagogue was forbidden by Jewish law from officiating at our wedding, he always held out his hands in welcome to both of us. I know he wanted to see Pete, me, and Josh at any one of his services, and I wanted to see us there too. There was just this knotty ball at the bottom of my ribcage pulling at me, a dark-hearted dread that held me back. Luckily, my parents had no objections to my choices, having gotten used to my sister's two marriages outside the faith. But it wasn't *my* parents I worried about. It was my son.

Should I really be worried? I asked myself. I was raising my son Jewishly, and my husband was helping me. When we lit Shabbos candles, Pete tried to sing along with us even though he didn't know a word of Hebrew. He sometimes came to synagogue and shared in all our holidays. The chance of him converting was slim to none, but I never asked for that and never felt it was relevant.

Yet, I still couldn't bring myself to go to a synagogue the night before the holiday and dance around the Torah, whether alone or with Pete and Josh. In the end, I chickened out and went to services by myself the next day, listening to congregants chant the last chapter of Torah called *Vezot Ha Berachah* ("This is the Blessing")—and start over with Genesis, or *Bereshith*.

I read through the Haftorah Vezot Ha Berachah:

Be strong and very courageous, to observe to do according to all the law, which Moses My servant commanded thee; turn not from it to the right hand or to the left, that thou mayest have good success whithersoever thou goest.

At least it wasn't saying something terrible would happen if you did skate right or left, though I wasn't going to count on that. I had no special excuses, really, for marrying out. Just the old Trifecta, love and friendship, and respect. Plus (she says, blushing), chemistry. I probably shouldn't put that in a chapter about Torah, but God help me, it was part of the equation—or God not help me, as the case may be.

My nerves persisted all through the service and for a day after. And then a week later, I got a letter in the mail from our rabbi. The letter was addressed to congregants who were, or were soon to be, married to someone who is not Jewish. It asked if we wanted to attend a meeting to find out how the synagogue can be most helpful to us.

I sat on my bed, reading it over. This was not my grandmother's rabbi, or my mother's, or even the one who performed the wedding ceremony with my former spouse. This was someone who understands that you can be Jewish and raise your children as Jews, and still not be married to a Jewish person. And instead of saying *get out of here*, he said, *come in and talk to me*. "How can I help?"

Did I still feel a little bit guilty? I'm Jewish, right? And I knew there were still many people who believed I did the wrong thing by getting married to Pete. But the rabbi's letter made me feel like I could be a good parent to the son of a cantor no matter who I'm married to, that there were ways we could pass our heritage on to our children even if we did move a little to the right and a little to the left.

Which is, as far as I was concerned, plenty reason to rejoice.

31

WHERE, JEWISHLY? THOUGHTS ON THE PEW SURVEY

I HAD JUST FINISHED reading a recent Pew Survey summary on how many Jews, especially young ones, are no longer identifying Jewishly. I was trying to decide how much identifying I did in my twenties—none at all, or very little—though I went to my parents' seders and lit candles for Hanukkah.

Oddly enough, my son's dad and I met at an audition in New York, and one of the first things he asked me was "Are you Jewish?" I'm still not really sure why he asked. But he did, we got together, got married, and had a son who decided to become a cantor like his dad, singing the liturgical prayers in a synagogue.

What does this mean for him and for his future? Are there fewer young people who identify Jewishly or are they just, well, young and not identifying with any religion? How many twenty-somethings go to church, anyway? And don't most people start going to a church or synagogue when they start having young children?

Or maybe there's less of them around too. I've read numerous articles about how less couples are getting married and having kids and how most people wouldn't describe themselves as religious.

Reading articles like these makes me think of my thirteenth year when I was supposed to have a bat mitzvah and didn't get one.

I'm still not sure if it was because of too much religion or not enough. The Orthodox day school I attended didn't do bat mitzvahs for girls, and once I left to go to public school, my parents didn't seem to think I needed one either. It seemed ironic that I was watching other thirteen-year-olds with no interest in living Jewishly celebrate their bat mitzvahs. What I remember about the two or three I got invited to were lavish parties with bands, dancing, and *kosher-style* food, which likely meant separating meat and dairy and holding off on pork or shrimp.

Would I have preferred to have a party like that? Not for the world. What I really wanted was to go back to my old school and be with my old Jewish classmates. I didn't want to be the princess for a day. I wanted everyday rituals and prayers, jokes in Hebrew, and everything that made my first school feel like home.

Years later, I found myself in charge of my own Jewish choices and had to parse out what they mean to me. On holidays with friends, I felt on top of the world, sharing rituals, food, Jewish stories. On other days, I thought, *why am I doing this*?

It's hard to be kosher, observe the Sabbath day, and say all the prayers in Hebrew. And I fall short, and short and shorter. So, then. Why?

Someone once said to me when speaking of Jewish life in Germany during the Nazi era, "What does it matter whether people thought of themselves as Jewish or practiced Jewishly then? They were killed for being Jewish. So, if nothing else makes you a Jew. . ."

Well, yes. Right (clears throat). But I'd like to have more positive reasons to identify myself as Jewish. Here's my partial list, as incomplete as it is:

- Holiday dinners or parties with friends and family
- Jewish music (sacred and secular)

- Kosher eateries, wherever I can find them
- Jewish rituals
- Jewish humor
- Jewish stories, plays, paintings, and films
- The music of prayer and the fact that prayers are chanted/musical
- The way we recognize each other, even when we don't say so
- Israeli chocolate
- My son's face when he is singing Jewish music

That's not to say that it's easy. Most Jewish people know that observance takes a lot of support, discipline, commitment, and sometimes way more money than it should. I'm not happy about that and I don't know what to do about it.

I have had Christian friends who said they envied Jews for the beauty and richness of their culture and religion. I wish I could ask them to explain that to other Jews, who don't seem to notice it at all. But I can't.

I do know I'd miss my heritage and tradition if it wasn't here. I feel lucky to have had the chance to raise a son Jewishly and to have learned more than I would have known otherwise. I don't know what to say to anyone else who is not Jewishly inclined. But I do know there's a very rich tapestry out there with a cultural stew that may not be as eternal as some of us might want to think. You won't miss it if you don't know about it. But a part of you *will* be missing. I know it would for me.

Like someone saying they would never want to see a foreign country or fall in love or have a child or build a house or go sailing, you can live just fine without all these things, but then there's always a part of you on the sidelines. Isn't there? A part that you aren't using or experiencing. Then what happens? And where does that part of you go—or not go?

Where, Jewishly? Where at all?

32

HANUKKAH, MISTLETOE, AND THE HILLEL RABBI

WHAT DECEMBER DILEMMA? *Ohhhh.* That one. After getting married in a civil ceremony, I had navigated two months with relative calm before bumping into the winter holidays. I thought the year before was complicated, but that was nothing compared to where we were headed.

Last year, Josh and I navigated the Christmas/Hanukkah celebrations with my sister. Things seemed much less fraught a year later without my sister's intense determination to put up a tree and tolerate our menorah lighting instead of participating in it.

This time, I set out the menorah and lit candles, and when we said the blessings, Josh showed his stepfather how to play dreidel. I watched them, thinking, *This is what I wanted, a husband who isn't just supportive of our traditions, but really is interested in them.*

But as Hanukkah ended and we started getting closer to Christmas, the dilemma approached us too. This was Pete's holiday, and he had not converted or given it up. Did he want a tree? I decided to ask. He said he had a tiny fake tree about twelve inches tall, and that is all he wanted. Was he trying to please me? Probably. I had no idea what to say or do.

I thought about Josh going over to his father's and talking about a Christmas tree at our house, and my face turned red at the thought. Why did I care? I remembered Josh's father's wife asking me once, when she heard I was dating, "Is this one Jewish?"

In her question, I could hear my ex's disapproval and worry about how Josh would be raised. At the same time, we all knew the ship had sailed and a Jewish husband wasn't on it. So, the answer was no, dear.

This one was not.

A few days before Christmas, I found myself in front of a florist's shop. When I opened the door, the smell of pine greeted me like one of those seductive aroma graphics you see in cartoons. I saw pine branches, holly, and mistletoe, which I remember from old movies where someone was always trying to get next to someone else.

I circled around the room, thinking of "*The Gift of the Magi*" story by O. Henry and trying not to cast myself in an overly romanticized version of it by substituting holidays instead of gifts for the self-sacrificing lovers. But the story and store ruined any chance I had of being rational.

O. Henry won.

I brought home a bagful of pine branches, holly, and mistletoe and arranged them around the room, thinking they might make a kind of alternative to a Christmas tree. I waited to see what Pete and Josh would say. Josh turned out to be easy. Ignoring everything else, he made a beeline for the Hanukkah candy known as *gelt* and peeled back the wrapping with eager fingers. Pete, on the other hand, seemed pleased with my decorations and found a way to maneuver me under the mistletoe. Which was fun, I must admit.

A few days later, presents arrived in the mail from Pete's parents. Josh's and mine said Happy Hanukkah and Pete's said Merry

Christmas. We opened our gifts next to a foot-high fake evergreen and later went to a movie—and that, I thought, was that.

Except it wasn't. Because two days later, my friend Shoshanna stopped by with her husband, who happened to be the Hillel rabbi at the local university. We were at the dining room table and the rabbi looked up, his eye catching the mistletoe.

"What is that?" he asked.

His wife, a convert who was originally named Sasha and born Episcopalian, replied too quickly. "You know what it is."

I blushed. And blushed. And blushed again.

I didn't say I was trying to find a way to share Pete's traditions without observing them. I hadn't gotten it right yet, but I wanted very much to figure it out. At the same time, I felt like Pete was bending a lot more in my direction than I was for him. Yet I still couldn't bring myself to want a tree and felt relieved when he didn't push it.

The next year, Pete's parents came out to their cabin in Two Harbors and invited us for the holiday. I knew there would be a tree and all the trimmings, but it didn't bother me. Because we were not at home, it felt like going to visit another family where Christmas is celebrated, and this made everything easier.

We continued to celebrate Hanukkah in our house, and Christmas at Pete's family cabin. Josh and I got to share their traditions and enjoy them. We celebrated Jewish holidays in a Jewish home and met our Christmas trees elsewhere.

You might also say that meant I wanted to have my cake and eat it too, and you might be right. Maybe I just came up against a line I couldn't cross, and it surprised me as much as anyone. It could have been how I was raised, or my parents' faces when they saw my sister's tree. Or it could be my way of rebelling against all the things so many Jewish people do to be like everyone else. Whatever it was said yes to kisses, but no to Christmas trees—though maybe not always to mistletoe.

33
SOMEWHERE TO GO

HE WAS NINETEEN when he heard they could free him. I don't know who the rescuer was because family stories can be murky, and my father was repeating the stories his father told him. He had been living in freezing barracks, getting up every day at the crack of dawn. "What was he doing?" I would ask. "Digging ditches, repairing roads?"

"He was playing the bugle," my father said. "Your grandfather had a talent for it and other instruments like the clarinet, which he played years later."

Most young Russians were in the Tsar's Army for a few years, but they kept Jews for a quarter of a century. How long would they have kept my grandfather?

He was the youngest boy in his family, and they scrimped and saved to bribe someone to get him out. Brothers, sisters, mother, father, who? I want to know but don't. All I know is he was my grandfather and somehow got away from an army that couldn't have been easy to escape. His last place of residence was somewhere called "Srezpe" in Russia, but I cannot find it on any maps. His name was Josef, changed later to Julius.

I don't know how the money came or who got it, but when it came, they were able to pay someone to spirit out their boy, spiraling through the Siberian landscape from safe house to safe house, and then somehow over the border to Germany.

His ship was in Bremen. Called the *Havel*, it brought him to Ellis Island on the last day of June in 1897. He walked off the boat with five dollars in his pocket, maybe the bugle too. He was a Klezmer musician, playing weddings and other celebrations in his youth. Clarinet, clavinet? I have no idea. Dark hair, eyes, spectacles, looking more like a scholar than a musician. They paid him in whiskey, giving him a taste for it at an early age that led to addiction and early death. He is reaching out his hand today, and I wish I could take hold of it with my own.

It was my sister who found him through the Ellis Island website, the only young man with our name on the *Havel* manifest. People still ask, "What kind of a name is Zark?" I usually smile and say, "*My* name." They ask if it was shortened, changed from Zarkowitz, or Zarkofsky, or even Zarkh. But according to the records at Ellis Island, my grandfather's name was simply Josef Zark.

I smile to think how his ship has the name of one of my favorite playwrights, Vaclav Havel. He was an outlaw too, before becoming president of the Czech Republic. My grandfather must have been in steerage, weaving and bobbing with the waves. Sickly? Strong? My sister doesn't know, either. My parents were quite a bit older than me; I never met any of my grandparents and had only heard vague stories about their lives. My grandfather walked off the boat and made his way somehow to Bayonne, New Jersey. He later met a young woman from Byelorussia, Esther Kaplan, with long red hair she could sit on and skin like a porcelain doll.

Because my grandmother's name is more common, it has not been as easy to locate news of her yet. My mother's parents' records are also still out there, somewhere, hard to identify because the name was changed from Polanski to Greenberg. Why? One always asks these questions, but answers are hard to nail down. My mother told me the inspector at Ellis Island said they had too many Polanskis that day and so the name was changed to Greenberg. Who knows if this is true?

Josef took the name Julius, thinking maybe it sounded more American. I am told he had a grocery store at one time and played at various parties when he could find the work. He and my grandmother had three sons—Sam and twins named Max and Harry. Max was my father and says he and Harry ran around like "wild animals." At one point their father made illegal whiskey on the roof, and my grandmother had to entertain the police while he tried to get rid of it. They found it, of course, and brought him to jail instead. Luckily, he had connections who got him home.

Julius, lucky Julius, where is your family? I cannot think what must have happened to them, and I am afraid they may have perished, either in pogroms or the Holocaust. I know they had only enough money to get Josef out of the country and the rest of them had to stay. Mother, father, sisters, brothers, cousins? Vanished now, like smoke.

I only heard about my grandfather's arrival in this country when my sister called to share her findings. We talked about him, and I tried to visualize him, but the man I saw in pictures is much older, and I began to realize he was still a teenager when he came over here.

After the call, I walked down the street crying, knowing I must be scaring children as they stopped and stared. I was thinking of this young man, having no chance to say goodbye to his family, hiding in basements or attics and finally reaching the ship that would take him to safety. But it was also to a place where he didn't know a soul. He would never see his family again. He must have thought of them, played his music for them, missed them. Did he write them? Did he dare?

In his play, *Angels in America*, Tony Kushner talks about a great journey taken by our ancestors from the old world to the new, and how we will never make the great journeys like they did. When I saw the play, I remember standing in a crowded line in the lobby at intermission and hearing someone say they were stuck in line. Then I heard someone else saying, "You're only stuck if you have somewhere to go," and the words have stayed with me.

My grandfather had somewhere to go.

Without his journey, I would not be here to write plays and stories and books like this one. My father would not have fought in World War II and come home to build a business in Jersey City, employing both himself and his twin brother. His older brother, Sam, would not have become a statistician at the Pentagon—and I wouldn't say I *really* had an uncle Sam in Washington. My son would not have grown up to be a singer and musician; my sister, with her sculptures and artist's vision, would be gone too.

My father used to tell me one story about my grandfather, over and over. "This is America!" he would say. "Everything will work out!" It always made me laugh, but I'm starting to think about it in another way; the journey to get here also cost my grandfather something. For the first time, I can begin to understand what it was.

He didn't know about us and will never know us. But I am sitting here with Josef/Julius Zark's name and my grandmother Esther's red hair. I stand on the corner, looking at the green Minnesota parkland at the end of my street. Pretending he is with me, for a minute there, in the road.

"My son has some of your music inside him and maybe I do too," I say. "I owe you everything and will never know you. But I feel your hand, Grandpa, or as we say, *Zayda* Josef. Reaching out for me in the dark."

34
FRUITS OF JERUSALEM

HIS FINGERS CLOSED around the fig, leaning in to sniff and lick. He wasn't sure what to think, but biting yielded nothing, and after a moment, he gave up.

Next a date, which, though sweet, had too rough a texture; then a chocolate raisin, wrinkled and familiar. To my five-year-old son Josh, this was Tu B'Shevat—some odd, asymmetrical fruit.

We were in the Jewish Community Center's childcare wing where Josh went three days a week while I worked. It was Tu B'Shevat, and when I came to take Josh home, his class was tasting Israeli fruit and learning about the holiday known as the New Year for Trees.

Josh didn't quite understand it, and it wasn't easy to explain. We knew that in Israel, the trees were probably starting to run with sap, and I imagined there was greenery poking its head out of the ground. Years before my son was born, I was in Jerusalem planting a tiny sapling. I looked at Josh, who was utterly done with dried Israeli fruits and signaling he was about to run off unless I started dressing him. I knelt to put his coat, scarf, hat, and boots on, wondering what he would remember about this holiday.

I celebrated Tu B'Shevat as a child in Hebrew day school, though I don't think chocolate raisins had been one of the fruits we ate. At Josh's age, I knew next to nothing about *Eretz Yisrael*, and when told, it seemed as exotic as fairyland to me, a made-up country floating somewhere next to the castles I saw in Disney movies. The idea of people fighting, dying, or even living normally there never occurred to me; if it was home to anything, it would have to be magic, like a dream.

The stories I heard from the Bible cemented this; Abraham and Sarah serving angels in their tent and having a child in old age; Jacob wrestling with an angel; the parting of the Red Sea; Lot's family turning into pillars of salt; Joshua blowing his horn while the walls of Jericho fell around him. Years later, I stood in a Jericho courtyard, listening to an archaeologist say that some scientists believed the walls were quite weak, but it wasn't until then that I began to apprehend the difference between the myths I'd grown up with and reality.

There is nothing like Israel to change the way you look at the country, but still, somehow, it comes out mythically, or at least seems to when you're visiting. The outsized Biblical figures from my youth towered over childhood like so many skyscrapers, yet when I arrived in Jerusalem, riding on a bus through the hills of the city's olive groves, it felt as though I'd traded one fairytale for another.

Here was a place where passion was palpable, where people, whatever their differences, seemed engaged with one another and themselves. For a woman who'd grown up in a place where most of us spent our days staring at TV screens, that in itself was a reason to stare.

My journal, day one:

The hills are arid, ancient, worn to patience; they look for no unexpected kindness from those who walk them. Yet kindness comes in unexpected ways. The land is dotted with lush green terraced gardens, rows of olive trees, and the stone houses that appear almost to be rising from the ground instead of squatting on it, as so many American houses do. It is lovely to see mountains again.

One can almost feel the history of this place, pouring out of trees and rocks and heartbeats. They have kept it alive, whatever else they might not have done; so that to see it, you have only to open your eyes. It's almost like the air itself can make you feel like you have been asleep for a long time and only just realized what it was to be truly awake.

As we drove home over snowy roads, I remembered my first week in Jerusalem—the city's music, stones, and air, all conspiring in a rush of heat and sensuality to knock out every other thought, life, relationship I'd ever had, to sweep me up into a lush, provocative now.

Day 3: They—and by that I mean everyone I'm seeing—live on the edge of life here; so they live more fully, because they take nothing for granted.

As Josh and I got into our driveway, whatever it was I felt in Jerusalem evaporated into the very circumscribed world of single parenthood. I pulled leftovers out of the refrigerator to make a casserole. Josh clattered around the kitchen, doing everything he could to get underfoot. My usual MO was to turn on the television, but on this night, I thought, *No.* If we were *really* present in our lives, I wouldn't turn on the TV. I would find some other way to engage him while I cooked dinner, and it wouldn't be by tuning him out.

I reached underneath the sink and pulled out three pots, then opened a drawer to find a spoon. "Here," I said, "bang on this and make some music." Josh took the spoon and began banging as though he'd rehearsed it a thousand times.

The symphony continued—bang, crash, bang, and boom. Listening to it, I began to understand. We were alive, Josh and I, like the fruits of Jerusalem. The trees, figs, noise, and clatter told us we are alive, and we cannot take it for granted.

We are here for a short time only, every day a kind of Tu B'Shevat saying you have to keep blooming, every fruit is a first fruit, and you can't be fallow too long. Behind each winter, spring arrives, and the stories won't wait. They are here, like the two of us, waiting on dinner—and the dawn.

35

EXPIRATION DATE ON JAPS IS LONG PAST DUE

I WAS SITTING in the audience of a local theater not long ago, watching new plays by young playwrights. *They are wonderful,* I thought, until the last one, which almost got me to leave early. While most of the audience seemed to be whooping it up, I was feeling more and more depressed.

The play's main character was a Jewish woman so completely caricatured she could only be called a Jewish American Princess (a.k.a. JAP). She had a fake New York accent and all the stereotypical trappings such women are supposed to have—great wealth, prudishness to match, and so on. In addition, she was racist and stupid in equal measure.

I don't believe the young author is anti-Semitic, and he certainly has plenty of company in creating Jewish female characters obsessed with money and themselves. But when I asked about the choices made in this play at a postshow discussion, I was told it was supposed to be about the prejudice inherent in all of us. Funny, I said, because the Jewish woman was the only person in the play who seemed prejudiced. *No other character made racist comments,* as far as I could see.

And do you, I asked, really think Jewish women are as obnoxious as the character you created? Do you realize I am a Jew?

"You're not a stereotypical Jewish woman," came the reply.

"So you think there *are* stereotypical Jewish women?" I said. "Who are *they*?"

I got no answer and was reluctant to press the point because it seemed pretty obvious we weren't getting anywhere. I also felt like if my son was there, he would have said, "So what, Mom? What's the big deal?" I tried to puzzle this out on the way home and had to admit that Jewish people too—men and women—have said they know people who fit these stereotypes.

Yet nowhere is the stereotype as prevalent as it is in movies and theater.

I suppose in some universes, Jewish American Princesses are funny. I have never found them so but since people in the audience were guffawing, I must be missing something. I couldn't help thinking how much funnier—and more dangerous and sexy—the play could have been, say, if the other characters had some quirks or flaws too.

Instead, the scenes were dominated by an ugly, female, Jewish cartoon. Because the image of the *JAP* is so persistent in our culture, no one even questions it—including Jews, I'm sorry to say. And if any other ethnic group was portrayed this way—as a Hindu or Muslim American princess, for example—wouldn't the audience be up in arms? They should be. Yet somehow Jewish women continue to be fair game.

Yeah, funny. The ones I know are vibrant, accomplished with advanced degrees, intelligent, curious, kind, disciplined, and talented. They are comfortable with their sexuality too, thank you. And yes, Virginia, we have our bad days, like everyone else.

But if young playwrights are so smitten with Jewish American Princess stereotypes now, what will they say about us when they're older? Isn't there something else we can put up as a counterweight to the stock figures we see onstage and in films?

I've heard people say you should take the words people use to label you and invert them so the labels have new meanings that transcend the old stereotypes. I've never tried that because to me it always seemed more reactionary than real. But it could be an interesting exercise. What do you think? Should I sign my name this way?

Jenna Zark

Jewish American Playwright (JAP)

Jewish American Professional

Jewish American Person

Sigh!

All of the above?

36

SON OF THE FAITH

HE WAS GONE; I was alone; I was holding his hand. In a few minutes I would be calling the funeral director, who would ask if I wanted a Jewish burial for my father. That meant he would be given a ritual washing by members of the Sacred Burial Society, called *Hevra Kadisha* in Hebrew. I would have to say yes or no.

My father was not even remotely religious and had not been since the rabbi at his Depression-era synagogue denied him a bar mitzvah because his family couldn't pay dues. Bar/bat mitzvah literally means *son/daughter of the commandments* or *the faith*. The ceremony is about joining the Jewish community, and Dad had always regretted missing out on it.

I looked down at my father's still-warm hand, trying to decide what to do. I could see him as a skinny, freckly twelve-year-old, blue eyes widening as he took in the rabbi's words. My father would have been smiling, because he didn't like letting people know when they hurt him. He would have shrugged and nodded quickly, turning away.

I tried to remember how I felt when I first heard of the Burial Society. Like many American Jews, I grew up knowing nothing of how our tradition treats the dead, and my introduction to it had not been an auspicious one. When Mitch first became a cantor, we moved to Hammond, Indiana, from New York, where we had been struggling actors and writers. He started his first job at a Hammond synagogue, and I began to write plays.

Mitch joined the Burial Society almost immediately, which came as a shock to me. He described it, almost offhandedly, as a group of "special people" who take care of the dead by washing and dressing them. The washing, called *tahara* in Hebrew, has been performed since ancient times in Jewish communities. It sounded weird and a little frightening, because beyond seeing one non-Jewish friend in his coffin, I had never been close to death. I wasn't sure how to react and asked him why he was joining.

Because he had never been in a war or had other intense life and death encounters, Mitch thought joining the Society would be an important experience for someone starting a career in the clergy. He also believed the Society was a group willing to do what no one else would—and that intrigued him.

I thought he was nuts. My mother and friends also thought he was nuts, but how could I tell him that? When I pressed for more details, he said he had something to show me. Instead of taking me to a funeral home, he brought me to a hair salon, where, to my surprise, he introduced me to the owner, who shook my hand and offered me a free haircut.

I watched her as she pumped my seat higher and placed her scissors out on the counter. Her name was Nancy, and she was a member of Mitch's congregation. She was close to my age, in her late twenties, with a fountain of long curly hair, tight black leather pants, and long red nails.

"I heard your husband is a member of the Hevra Kadisha," she said as she lifted my hair while grinning into the mirror. Then she leaned over and whispered, "Me too."

I looked up at her as she smiled. Those slender white fingers with

perfectly polished nails were going out at night and washing dead
people. What's more, they were people Nancy knew. As she started
cutting and layering, I knew I had to learn more.

The Hevra Kadisha comprises volunteers from every community
and profession. They are hair stylists, secretaries, lawyers, wives and
mothers, fathers, bakers, salesmen, nurses, and students. They can be
called at any time, day or night, because in Jewish law, the dead must
be buried within twenty-four hours whenever possible. They give up
weekends, evenings, and holidays to do this holy work.

Typically, the washings are done by funeral-home staff because
the volunteer pool for groups like these is drying up. But in some
communities like Hammond or Minneapolis, sacred burial societies
are coming together at the request of local rabbis and retrieving the
Hevra Kadisha from obscurity. Each member will tell you something
different about why he or she joined.

Nancy became a member to try and make sense of her aunt's
death from cancer. The ritual she described was one I too would
come to know, some years later. The washing takes place on a simple
slab or platform and is done with a washcloth and basin. The person
on the slab is generally covered with a large white sheet or cloth.
Society members wash their hands three times in a ritual basin and
say a prayer, asking for kindness for the body.

Then, little by little, each body part is uncovered and lovingly,
carefully washed. A foot, a hand, a finger, forehead, shoulder. After
each part is uncovered to be washed with a washcloth, it is covered
again to be sure the person who is dead retains the highest amount
of dignity. At the same time, prayers are said from the Song of Songs.

*Her body is as polished ivory overlaid with sapphires. Her legs are
pillars of marble set upon foundations of fine gold. Her mouth is
most sweet, and she is altogether precious . . .*

Meanwhile, those doing the washing are experiencing a very

intimate relationship. Because the dead are so heavy and cannot bend, the people washing them must get very close to the body to lift and clean it thoroughly. You are near enough to feel and smell the body, and in doing so, you learn that you are not so very far apart, after all. They are like us—a bit colder, but not half as cold or stiff or strange as you may have been led to believe.

When everything has been washed, the body is strapped down. The platform or slab is raised so the body is in a vertical position, and three buckets holding eight quarts of water each are poured over the body in rapid succession. Those present who are living call out, *"Hu tahare"* or *"Hee tahara"*—meaning he or she is pure.

Perhaps it is to connect the dead with the living, symbolically. Perhaps it is to wash away all the sorrows, mistakes, or baggage they carried in life. I don't know exactly, but I do know the care lavished on the deceased is to show as much reverence for the body as the soul. Because the body is the home where the soul resides, the washing is our last chance to say goodbye.

When the washing is over, the deceased is lowered and dressed in a white linen shroud. The pants are tied four times around the waist, and then a top is put over them. The shroud has no pockets, so you take nothing out of this world. The prayers continue and a bag of earth that contains soil from Israel is sprinkled around the body. Next, pottery is placed over the eyes and mouth. A cotton sash is tied around the waist to spell the letter *shin*—used to symbolize the name of God.

By the time I saw the tahara, we had moved from Indiana to Minneapolis and the rite was performed at a local funeral home. Nancy and I stayed in touch, and not long after, I decided to make my friend the pivotal character in a play about this ritual.

The day I visited, two older women were being washed by three people. The youngest smiled at me and said, "I do this in the hopes that someone will be there to do it for me."

As I watched the Hevra Kadisha members dressing the bodies,

a flood of memories from the years I spent in Hammond returned. I remembered how Mitch would come home after a washing to say the person he took care of was a congregant. He would describe how it felt to put a shroud over the head of a man who had been joking with him only a few days before. I couldn't help wondering what effect this was having, and if it would be traumatic, but it seemed to be the opposite. Ultimately, I think it made him more comfortable with death and, in an altogether different way, in his own skin.

Another society member named Ursula told me about a mother who lost her little girl. Because she knew Ursula was a member of the Society, the mother called her to ask if the child could be buried in her shoes. "She will be cold," the mother said, weeping. "How can I bear it if my little girl is cold?"

On hearing this, Ursula wept too. "Of course," she said, knowing that while burials are supposed to be done without shoes, it was more important to respect the mother's wishes. "That was the time I was most glad to be in the Hevra Kadisha," said Ursula, "because this lady could call and talk to me. She did not have to deal with some faceless funeral home. She knew we would love and care for her daughter as we would our own."

When we left the tahara in Minneapolis, we washed our hands in a basin outside the door. This was meant to signify that we were, once again, rejoining the land of the living. What struck me most about this experience was that in normal life, we are all so divorced from death. We never think about it unless it happens to a close friend or relative. Yet I can't help but feel that in the past, our grandparents and their parents had stronger ties to life and each other because of this ritual.

Remembering all this, I called the funeral director and told him I wanted to give my father a traditional Jewish burial. When I hung up, I again took Dad's hand in my own. I thought of what he'd say if he knew what I was planning. *"What are you doing here? Don't you know your own father?"* I thought of how rabbis in my father's generation were often small and narrowminded and how quickly they made decisions that affected people for years to come. *"But maybe that's the point,"* I wanted to say. No rabbi has the power to give or take away what is yours.

And so, they washed him. I was not present, was not allowed to be, as family members are prohibited from attending the washings of relatives, but I knew they were holding him, bending their faces to his, and sprinkling the dark Israeli earth around his eyes. I could feel the gentleness in their hands as they covered him with buckets of water, one, two, three, in a continuous stream of clean and cold. They would be saying, in their prayers, that he belonged, that he was pure, that his soul was Jewish, and that he was, finally and forever, bar mitzvah—a son of the faith.

37

WHEN YOU HAVEN'T GOT A PRAYER—MAKE ONE

BEFORE YOU HIT the ice cream, couch, magazine, and Dr. Pepper— are you gonna pray? I'm asking myself this because I already know the answer—*doubt it.*

When I was a newly divorced single mom, I prayed all the time. Every day, twice a day, in Hebrew and English, morning and evening. I said conventional prayers and then more personal ones, the *Shema,* the *Amidah* prayer, *Hallel,* and others. I promised God that if I could find a job and a better life, I'd pay it forward. I can't prove that praying helped, but I feel like it did. And then things got better; I found a job, met a great guy, got married, and found myself praying less and less—except at stressful times or when I made it to synagogue.

At Yom Kippur services one year, I brought a friend to synagogue with me. She was from Panama and had always felt Jewish growing up but could never prove it. She converted formally later and—maybe naturally—was more excited about things Jewish than most of us. As on every Yom Kippur, the prayers went on for quite a while. At a certain point, I looked over at my friend and said, "A lot of prayers today, huh?" She looked back at me, smiling. "He deserves it."

Hearing her say that made me think. *What is really happening when we pray*? When I open the *siddur* (prayer book) and look at the Hebrew letters, I feel like they're sort of an anchor. I learned these letters and words as a first grader in day school, and they will always be a part of me. What I love about the ancient prayers is they've been recited and chanted for generations.

What I don't like about the prayers is the same thing—they've been recited and chanted for generations, and who knows what we are saying, anyway? They may be beautiful as the psalms by King David usually are. But when he was writing them, they meant something to him. Try as I might centuries later, I can find no passion and no song, in short, nothing that moves me and makes me want to do much of anything—let alone continue praying.

When I was little, I learned all the morning prayers by heart at school. The *Ashrei*, *Shema*, and *Aleinu* were like second nature and second skin. On weekends, though, I rarely prayed—unless something bad happened. One night I watched *Chiller Theatre* with my older sister and saw a movie about a cyclops that scared me so badly I couldn't sleep. My parents were surprised to see me praying away fiercely the next morning bright and early at 7 a.m.—even at age eight, I tended to be a night owl. But I was just too frightened not to pray.

Yet I don't want to pray because I'm frightened. I want something more out of praying—something that will take me to a stronger way of seeing or enduring or being. But where do I start?

Hasidim tell a story about Rabbi Yisrael Baal Shem Tov, the founder of the Hassidic movement in the eighteenth century who was trying to put more joy and feeling into prayer. He went to a large synagogue in a strange town with some of his followers. The Baal Shem Tov looked inside the synagogue, which was very big and fancy, and said, "There is no space for me in there." His followers looked inside and said, "Master, there are plenty of empty seats and it's time to pray. Please! Let's go in." But the Baal Shem Tov said,

"The people in this synagogue don't really care about praying, so the prayers can't take wing and fly to HaShem. They're just empty words and they fall to the floor, which is full of them. They're everywhere, so I can't go in there. There isn't room for me."

I'm not Hasidic and I probably wouldn't follow the Baal Shem Tov even if he was here with me. But I get his point. Those empty words are lining the walls and floor of our synagogues, and until we really start praying, there won't be much room for us. But if we could pray, I mean, really care about praying and pray like we care, what would those prayers look like?

I have had friends—and I know you have too—ask for prayer chains on behalf of people who are seriously ill or in terrible accidents. There are times when I've been involved in those chains and heard the prayers worked and the people recovered. If prayers have power for occasions like these, what about for the rest of our lives?

When I think of prayers that really reach me, I think of music and songwriters that make me stop whatever it is I'm doing and listen. Leonard Cohen, Paul Simon, Baaba Maal, Johnny Clegg, Sinead O'Connor, Alison Krauss, Beethoven, Brahms, Bach, and Rachmaninoff. Honestly, though, the music doesn't make me think at all; it just brings me out of myself, out of the wide yawning canyon I fall into now and again when fear and fatigue take over. It tells me there's a way out and a way in, and I don't have to be afraid if I don't want to. It tells me there are things inside us that need to be articulated, alive, and waiting to be recognized.

This year, there were many reasons I needed to pray again—especially concerning illness and the people I love. At my synagogue, we say a special prayer requesting healing on behalf of family or friends called the *Mi Shabeirach*. My favorite version is sung by the late Debbie Friedman, and if you can find it online, I think you'll see why. To me it has everything the best prayers need to have—longing, love, passion, and compassion. It has become the model for how I judge every other prayer.

Were you ever able to find a prayer like that? If you have, I hope you'll send it to me at *jennazark.com*. I want to hear it. I want to say it—and I want it to be ours. *Our words. Our thoughts. Our music.* What prayers do you want to say and want your children to say? If you were in charge of sending prayers to God, what would you want to hear? If you had only one prayer you could say and it was the last thing you could ever say, what would it be?

Maybe that's what's missing from the Judeo/Christian liturgies— prayers that really move us because they are our own. My friend from Panama was right, I think, when she said, "He deserves it."

So do we.

38

NOT MY UNCLE'S SEDER

SHE WAS MY SON'S FIRST CRUSH, and favorite babysitter. Katherine looked like a teenager, though she was twenty-something when we met. I think she must have liked horror movies because Josh impressed her by quoting the 1930s movie *Dracula*.

"This kid is my kind of people," she told me after Josh asked her to come into his parlor in a Bela Lugosi voice. They were at his father's synagogue.

More than monsters, Katherine liked football, cats, and especially the Vikings. When Josh entered junior high and started playing for his school's football team, Katherine came to watch and, unlike his mother, knew all the plays. Something else she knew was how to make a seder shine, pop, and stick in your mind, even days and weeks later.

As a child, I knew just one kind of seder, sitting around a table with my aunt's best dishes and tablecloth. Our Haggadah guidebooks were the regulation yellow and red standard issue, and we watched my uncle Irving read aloud, occasionally allowing those who knew Hebrew to join him. My cousin Johnny and I were bored out of our skulls but neither one was brave enough to raise a distraction; we would have paid dearly and knew it.

When I moved to the Midwest with Josh's dad, we hosted seders that mostly emphasized singing, which made sense since Josh's father was a cantor. When single again, I was invited to festivities where others, like me, were experimenting, trying to make a long, ancient ritual come alive. There is a saying that we are all still escaping from Egypt, but for many years, all I could think of when I heard that saying was—I want to escape right *now*. I changed my mind because of Katherine and her seder when Josh was ten.

Katherine was Jewish but had not been raised as a Jew. I think someone in her family might have been, though she can trace her ancestry back to a minor prince who came to England with William the Conqueror—and both parents' families came over on the Mayflower.

While there is no one event or story that brought her to Judaism, she said she did begin to feel a kind of kinship with the rituals and traditions. One day she did something about it by formally converting and joining a synagogue. I'm not sure what this has to do with the quality of her seders, but it might be that she had traveled a long distance to find these rituals and they, too, had been waiting for her. The energy between them ignited a stronger spark.

I found this energy when I brought my son to Katherine's apartment on the first night of Passover. It wasn't any one thing she did, but it may have been the flow of things. A plateful of vegetables passed around throughout the evening so we wouldn't get hungry; a way of drawing out the kids at her table so they talked in ways I'd never heard them before; a scattering of rubber bugs and frogs and creepy crawly *plagues* all over the table.

She asked Josh and his friend Ari to pretend they were Pharaoh and Moses and to give us an idea of what they might have said in the final hours before the Hebrews escaped. Like all good teacher/ directors, she made suggestions while they were acting that spurred their imaginations and made their arguments stronger. And when things got too serious, she got us throwing rubber bugs at each other during the recitation of plagues and smacking each other with bitter herbs.

The adults got to chime in too, of course, but I have always found most seders talk down to children, though they pretend to be engaging them. On this holiday night, I got to watch my son come out of his ten-year-old shell because Katherine teased the questions out of him, dancing on the edge of his imagination until he figured out what he wanted to say. More; she made him feel important saying it. Yet what I remember most from that night was the sound of people laughing.

Something happens when someone has a chance to light on a ritual one feels deeply connected to but may not have known as a child—a new way of seeing and apprehending. Katherine had spent years collecting pieces of Haggadahs she liked and assembling them into her own Passover story. She found the music inside the seder and instinctively made it move, like a fish in a silver river.

If Seders really are for children, Katherine won them handily to her side. If they are for the child in all of us who believes in the strong hand and the outstretched arm, and in babies saved from drowning, we could probably do a lot worse than approaching a seder like we were new to it, too.

Watching Josh that evening, I finally understood the saying about all of us escaping from Egypt every time the story is told. It's very likely we are all trying to escape from something—maybe a job we hate or a sarcastic friend or relative—or just the little cruelties we see every day and try to ignore. And finding the courage to leave can be daunting without the story of someone who did it before you.

Not too long ago, I was lucky enough to be at Katherine's table again. Funny how things go full circle when you least expect it. Her seders continue to be like her life, unearthing discoveries in stories we've all heard over and over and turning them into something new.

Those discoveries make you feel braver, somehow, about the possibility of freedom, or taking risks you've always been afraid to take. They make me realize I may still be looking for a little more freedom too (not least from my own demons) and, yeah, the courage to find it. Maybe this year, I will.

39
NOT TO PLAY

WHEN MY SON JOSH said he had decided to be a cantor, I wanted to encourage him as much as possible. Schooling went very well, at least from my vantage point, but there were some relationship bumps I could only observe, helplessly, as there was nothing I could do about them.

Being a member of any clergy family has its challenges, but I know for certain being the wife of a cantor or rabbi can throw up roadblocks you never anticipated. For Josh, that meant falling in love with women who wanted to love him back but couldn't stomach the idea of meeting the expectations they'd face from congregants.

I kept telling Josh he'd find the right person and not to rush it, but I also knew whoever he chose would have to navigate the treacherous waters of being held to account for what she said, did, ate, cooked, and wore—sometimes on a daily basis.

For me that meant episodes I could have done without— including an incident that happened when I was new to the Twin Cities and my ex-husband's congregation.

In the early days of settling into a new life and synagogue, the weather had been warm. Though I wore long skirts in synagogue (and we're talking ankle length here), I was not wearing hose with my sandals. Just before a brunch with friends, I opened a letter with a brief note:

Dear Madam,
At this Temple, we wear stockings.

It was unsigned, but the handwriting, according to the rabbi, made him believe the note was written by an older adult from another country. Whoever it was never came forward, though she (he?) did succeed in making me cry that day.

Over the years, I received other critiques, some well-meaning, others not. I overheard the president of the synagogue say something about how my dress exposed too much back and arms on Rosh Hashanah. (Why she was so worried about that on a Day of Awe is beyond me.) Others criticized me for not volunteering more, and still others had their opinions about my son and whether he should be allowed (or not allowed) at services.

But nothing anyone said while I was married came close to what they said when I was in the midst of a divorce. According to whatever sources you gossiped with, I was returning to New York and leaving (or taking) my son because I was overly ambitious, didn't like being married, or hadn't wanted children.

Some years after the divorce, I visited the synagogue for my son's bar mitzvah. Many people came up to greet us warmly, and that made me feel a bit more comfortable. Yet, throughout the morning, I was sure some people continued talking about me.

I don't mean to suggest that this is the only synagogue in the world where gossip occurs. We all do it—sure. But do we really need it in places where we're supposed to be connecting to God? How, exactly, does that make things better for us or our kids?

In an earlier chapter, I mentioned that the Hebrew word for

gossip is lashone hara. The literal translation for that phrase is *evil tongue.* To me, that means what you are saying will leave a bad taste not only in your mouth, but in the mouths of people hearing you.

Yet isn't this one of the easier behaviors we can change? When it comes to what we say, don't we have a choice? If something bugs us about a friend, you can share it with that friend—hopefully respectfully. Why not try it with clergy? Can we possibly imagine they want to make congregants happy—and they're just as human as the rest of us?

I know my son will encounter this—and the person he loves will, too. No doubt the children he has will also have the weight of his position around their little shoulders. I haven't been asked to weigh in on this for a while, but if I was, I would just say—*what*?

I guess I'd say what I learned from being a cantor's wife. Go home. Ask Alexa to play Linda Ronstadt's version of "People Gonna Talk," or play it yourself as loudly as possible. Dance around the room and, if you have kids, get them to dancing too.

Comments, expectations, whispers will come and go. Dance anyway.

The only way to win is not to play.

40

LETTER TO A GUM BANDIT

SOMEWHERE BETWEEN LAST SHABBAT and this one, my gum and a teenager's story got connected in a very nasty way. On Tuesday morning, I opened the door of my car, turned on the ignition, and was about to hit the radio button when I noticed it wasn't there. Instead, my dashboard was corkscrewed sideways, and the front piece of my radio was on the seat, along with the surrounding panel. The door to my glove compartment was on the floor.

I hadn't locked the garage the night before. I was having trouble with the service door and thought, *Why bother?* My neighborhood was generally placid, and wouldn't it be too cold for people to go prancing around looking for stuff to steal? We were supposed to be heading into the coldest night of the year. I pressed the lock button on my car—or at least I thought I did. But if I had, none of this would have happened.

Someone walked inside the garage, opened the car door, and tried to grab what he/she could. Later on, a policeman said my burglar was probably a male kid who couldn't get the CD player out fast enough and decided to move on to the next garage. Which he did, a few doors down, and then stole a moped.

The policeman helped me get my dashboard straight again and set the radio panel back where it's supposed to be. But after he left, I sat in the car a while, thinking. I have been thinking ever since, as Shabbat approaches, about this visit.

In my mind's eye, my visitor was about sixteen. I'm tending to agree he was a guy because, being the parent of a son, it seems to me that boys tend to take more risks (or am I being old fashioned?). He didn't take my phone or CD player. But when I looked down at the seat, I saw my gum was gone.

He left the cold-weather snacks—raw peanuts and pecans—and instead swiped my Extra pack of gum. My husband said the thief must have realized he lacked the tools to remove the CD player. This was likely his first burglary. Maybe he was with friends, but I think he was alone.

I tried to picture this while getting ready for Shabbat. It's a day I've come to appreciate more and more lately, a time to light candles, see friends, have dinner with friends and family. A precious time when I am working on what seems like a million projects with very little time left for anything else. When I was younger, I used to wonder about the Torah commandment, "Remember the Sabbath and keep it holy." Now I think it's not us keeping the holiday; Shabbat is keeping us.

But Shabbat wasn't what my burglar was thinking about, I know. How cold was it in my garage on Tuesday morning? What time was this person there? What was he wearing? Why was he there? I don't want to meet him, but for ten minutes, the ten minutes he was in my garage at least, I want to *be* him. To see and understand what he was doing there. Because he took my gum, and that tells me something about him. Something hungry and lonely—something sad.

I should be no stranger to burglaries. I can't swear to it but think most of the people whose houses or cars are broken into tend not to be rich, because rich people have better protection—gated communities, dogs, and alarms. In New York, my apartment was broken into at least twice. I kept cash inside my bookcase, hoping thieves wouldn't find all of it. That didn't work, and I had to find a series of hiding places for the entire time I lived at that place.

My favorite robbery story occurred on the subway a few nights before I moved to the Midwest. I had a purse and one of those *shleppy* bags New Yorkers always carry around with them, since most of us don't have cars and have to shlep our stuff around. On this particular night, my bag held some Dead Sea salts and a magazine with Nelson Mandela on the cover. I was distracted, thinking of all the things I needed to do before moving, so I boarded an empty car that was dimly lit.

When a young man walking through the cars saw me, he must have thought I was an easy mark. He grabbed my bag and ran to the next car before I could even register what had happened. I looked down, realizing that my purse was still intact, and had to smile. When I told a friend about the robbery, she grinned. "Dead Sea salts and Nelson Mandela. He had all the world in his hands and didn't know it."

Jewish law asks us to give to others in a tradition we call *tzedakah*. It's meant to help people in need as we get closer to Shabbat, and to help others anyway, whenever we can. But you can't give everything to everyone. You can't make everything better. And sometimes you aren't even asked.

The burglar got my gum; I got a story. He got cold. I got fear and anger, curiosity, and something else I can't explain. At my table on Shabbat, I am still thinking about him, wondering if he is having any kind of dinner, if he's with family or friends, if he is alone.

There are prayers I am saying that I know how to say because I learned them early, prayers that ask for healing, blessings over bread and wine, praises for the holiness of rest that sets it apart from days we spend working. I know prayers cannot protect you, but they can keep you safe. Not safe from burglary, but from the kind of anxiety that descends on us every day. Prayers and Shabbat teach us that we are part of a community, a strong community that has meant a lot to me.

The police say they found the moped, abandoned in a parking lot less than a mile from here. Maybe that means the burglar felt bad about stealing it; I hope he did. I see him taking off his shoes, maybe putting on slippers. Does he even have slippers? I see him sitting at a table with candles and a dinner with family and friends. People who listen and laugh when he talks and give him somewhere to go besides visiting my car at 2 a.m. Where he gets some bread, maybe a blessing. Something more for him to chew on besides my gum.

That is what I wish for him as the weather warms and people unlock their garages, homes, and hearts. Shabbat Shalom.

41

BEFORE THEY GO CRAZY

I WAS STANDING with a friend during a bar mitzvah one Saturday morning, as a thirteen-year-old teen took on the spiritual obligations of a Jewish adult. The bar mitzvah is a really big deal in Jewish families, so it was with interest that I heard my friend, who was not Jewish, describe the event she was seeing.

"I think this whole thing is such a brilliant idea," she said. I looked at her, squinting.

"Huh?"

"You honor your children just before they go crazy," she said, and I laughed, thinking of all the parents I knew trying to navigate the highwire act of raising teenagers. Of course, a bar mitzvah is about becoming part of a Jewish congregation and leading it—but I had to agree with my friend about twelve- and thirteen-year-olds entering the land of adolescent angst. On this particular morning in synagogue, I was expecting and did not even want to imagine my kid's bar or bat mitzvah. Instead, I turned my attention back to the bar mitzvah boy chanting his Torah portion.

And then one day, not quite knowing how I got there, it was

time for my own son's bar mitzvah, only instead of honoring him before *he* went crazy, I think all the adults around him went crazy instead. It was supposed to be the best of times, but the months and weeks leading up to Josh's bar mitzvah had been chaotic. Josh's stepmother, whom he loved deeply, had become ill with cancer and died. His younger siblings were in second grade and mourning their mother after months of watching her fight her disease. Josh's father was fighting to keep everyone afloat, including himself.

I, on the other hand, was struggling with my own demons, one of them being the belief that Josh preferred his father's family to mine. Throughout his childhood and well before his stepmother's passing, it felt like he wanted to be at his dad's more than he wanted to be with Pete and me. To be fair, there was a piano, guitar, singing, and brother-sister twins at the other house. While we brought Josh to museums, movies, and plays, I think it was simply more fun at his dad's place. Besides, as the books all say, boys want to be with their fathers more as they approach adolescence. My demons hadn't read the books, so even though I knew all this rationally, I opened the door to the green-eyed monster and let him waltz right in.

That's probably why, a few days before the bar mitzvah at his father's synagogue, Josh and I had a fight that reduced me to a teary mess. To his credit, Josh's father called later to see how I was doing. Somehow, he got us both laughing, and a few minutes later, I apologized to Josh. I had hoped it made him feel better, but I spent the evening obsessing about all my parenting mistakes.

By the time the morning prayers started on the day of the bar mitzvah, our extended family had assembled at the synagogue, looking up at Josh on the *bimah* (platform) as he began chanting the *parsha*, the Torah portion for the week. Each parsha is subdivided into chapters, and during a bar/bat mitzvah, the celebrant—age thirteen for most, age twelve for girls in Conservative and Orthodox synagogues—reads several chapters aloud in Hebrew.

Each chapter is read—chanted, really—from the Torah, a parchment scroll in Hebrew that's written by a specially trained scribe. The words in the Torah scroll have no vowels, which makes it difficult to read.

Josh's parsha was called *Behaalotecha,* meaning "when you light" or "when you kindle," which is fitting as it begins with Moses' brother Aaron being commanded to light the menorah in the Tabernacle (sanctuary).

Torah portions are set according to the calendar, so there's no choosing of one's portion. The kids do have the choice, though, of how many chapters to read and how many to offer to others. Josh decided to read all seven, which made his father beam as he stood next to Josh on the bimah.

I saw what it meant to Josh to be performing this ritual alongside his dad. Watching them together showed me how much it was helping Josh grow and how silly it was to want him to divide his time equally between us, as if he were a math equation.

As Josh read, I started following along with the English translation to better understand what he was saying in Hebrew. He had shared very little with me up to that point, studying his parsha only with his father. I hadn't done much reading on my own—mostly due to time constraints more than anything.

The opening chapters were straightforward enough—and pretty boring—with the tribe of Levi being initiated into the sanctuary service. Instructions followed and things built slowly, with details about celebrating Passover and the building of the Tabernacle. This signaled the start of the people's journey into Israel and moved into the two final chapters, where things finally started to get interesting.

As soon as the Jews set off for the Promised Land, they began grumbling about the difficulties of the journey and wished they were back in Egypt—insanity, considering they had been slaves there for four hundred years. They hated the manna provisions they were given and longed for meat. God's response was to promise an abundance of meat to the Jews until it comes out of their noses and nauseates them. I smiled slightly, thinking of how my mother would rail at us if we complained about her dinner menu.

In the final chapter, everyone's gloves were off. God provided piles of quail and the people devoured it eagerly. Those who ate most gluttonously died in a plague with the meat still stuck in their teeth.

We then move from bad to worse. Moses' brother Aaron and their sister Miriam spoke against their brother's decision to marry a Cushite woman who was not a Hebrew. God retaliated by striking Miriam with leprosy, which she endured for seven days, though Aaron was not punished for any of this. (*Why* am I not surprised?!) Moses pleaded with God to stop afflicting his sister and eventually Miriam was cured.

Though it's a horrifying story, I couldn't help but feel it was a perfect chapter for us on this bar mitzvah day. Seeing how the Jewish people erupted at Moses and how his siblings talked behind his back made me think of other Biblical stories and families. No matter how much we might think of people in the Bible as *elevated*, the truth is they were flawed human beings. Maybe the Torah is trying to tell us that it's not the people who matter, but their stories, journeys, and what they learned. Or didn't learn. Or forgot.

I finished the parsha and began following along with Josh as he continued chanting. His voice was already a confident baritone, and though a few cracks appeared, he recovered quickly. I remembered what my friend said about honoring your kids before they go crazy and decided, if Moses, Aaron, and Miriam muddled through, we could weather whatever might be coming our way, too.

When it came time to speak to Josh in front of the congregation, I talked about his persistence, courage, and kindness while he watched me silently. It was getting harder and harder to tell what he was thinking, and that was, I knew, something thirteen-year-olds were good at. I hoped we'd be lucky enough to celebrate many more occasions with each other, so he'd come to know how proud I was of him. And no matter what happened to him or with him or around him, I hoped nothing would keep him from being the man he was starting to become.

42
THE CANTOR'S SONG

THE SOUND WAS WIDE AND DARK—mixing rain and tears with salt and fire below the surface. I don't know what my son Josh thought of it, but he seemed to be riveted listening to his father sing. He was only two and didn't know what singing was, and it would be a while before I could explain that his father was a cantor, singing a cantor's song.

His father studied privately with a blind cantor in New York City, learning tropes and liturgical permutations until he could take a test at the United Synagogue of America. His teacher was an older man, sometimes cranky, often funny, always stubborn, and very proud. One day a hurricane enveloped the city and Josh's dad rushed over to the cantor's home to see if he was all right. The cantor told him to go home; it wasn't time for his lesson yet.

As a toddler, Josh watched his dad singing on the bimah at the front of the sanctuary. He was singing part of the liturgy, and though here and there the congregation joined him, often people stopped to listen instead.

Friends tend to remark on the Jewish tradition of singing

prayers throughout the service. Because I have prayed this way since childhood, I hardly ever think about it. But when I visit churches, it seems their hymns are sung only at prescribed times, and I think, *How can they remember the prayers? I learned them by heart because I learned to sing them.*

As Josh grew up, he talked alternately about becoming a boxer, fireman, soldier, and then a singer. At some point in college, he decided he wanted to be a cantor and applied to cantorial school. He had originally decided to audition for opera companies, and then backed out of that notion. Was it because he wanted more security? I am not really sure, but suspect it was more than that. While he often said, "I am not my father," I think he had always loved watching his father sing and finally felt confident in his ability to be his own kind of cantor. His voice had grown into a dark-chocolate fire, and when he and his dad sang together, it was like listening to twin oaks calling out and responding.

But while his father came to the profession without having to attend graduate school, things seem to have changed. Josh had about five years of graduate school ahead of him and a boatload of debt to accrue before the Cantor's Assembly would help him find employment.

When I told people this, they said it seemed almost like a medical school, and I agreed but didn't understand why. Later I came to find out that students had to know music theory, Jewish liturgical singing, and Hebrew, and learn how to offer pastoral care. Josh had studied vocal performance at a music conservatory and was comfortable with music and theory skills. As a cantor, he would need to learn numerous styles of *davening* (praying), involving singing the liturgical prayers for each holiday and Shabbat.

Once graduated, what does a cantor do? Years ago, cantors were expected to lead congregants in prayer and perhaps help prepare students for their bar and bat mitzvahs. Now cantors are not only teaching bar and bat mitzvah students, but they are also leading choirs, leading prayer services for mourners, leading services at weddings and funerals, and providing pastoral care.

The old blind cantor told us when I was married to Josh's dad that a cantor must be perfect. Every law broken by congregants must be upheld and observed by their cantors. I saw this when I was married to one.

The blind cantor did *not* say the congregation would fire one of its best rabbis because some board members didn't think he was "friendly enough." Nor did he tell us that when we divorced, the congregation would gossip incessantly. But he did explain that every rule on Shabbat, and every other holiday, must be observed, everything that went into our mouths must be kosher, and that congregants would be watching and waiting to see if we made a mistake.

I told my son it would be the same way for him. He understood and was willing to try.

But *there was something else* every cantor needs to do, the old blind cantor told us. I can't tell you, he said, because you either know it or you don't.

I believe my son *did* know, which is why he most wanted to become a cantor. He also knew before he started his career that he had to run the gauntlet of five years in graduate school—and find a way to pay for it as well. Another essay might also address the high cost of Jewish education, though I suspect every graduate specialty is going to have a high price tag one way or another. But I just don't know enough to explain why becoming a cantor costs so much—in money and time.

Josh understood he was facing a life of service and a congregation that upholds its ideals more than its reals. Yet. He wanted to become a cantor, and I said, *Good for you.*

What I still want to know is how people who are going to synagogue perceive their cantors. My synagogue, for example, relies heavily on its rabbi, but members of the congregation perform the liturgy, and people seem to be just fine with that. Yet I've seen congregations that wouldn't think of going without a cantor, also called *Shaliach Tzibur*—the messenger of prayer and leading voice of the liturgy.

Why would you need or want a messenger? Some people say it's because everyone in the synagogue wants to pray at their own pace and you need a cantor to be sure everyone starts and ends together. Others say it's undemocratic and we shouldn't look for intermediaries. But I think the ancient melodies—older than fire and the Temple Mount itself—sound differently when sung by a cantor who has dedicated his life to them.

What I hear when Josh and his father and other cantors sing is a *cri de coeur*; except instead of the heart, it sounds more like the soul, crying out to be heard by God through centuries of suffering. What I hear is the cantor pleading and calling and praising and above all saying, "We are here. We have not deserted you, so do not let us go. Do not abandon us."

This, I think, is what the old cantor was talking about when he said there was something he could not explain that every cantor needs to do.

No. It's not what I think.

I'm sure of it.

43

MADE BY TORAH

DOES TORAH MAKE YOU HAPPY? I don't mean this to be cynical
or a trick question. But on the Simchat Torah holiday (literally
meaning happiness of Torah), shouldn't we ask?

I belong to a synagogue where people take turns reading Torah,
people who aren't rabbis and don't have to read. I am proud of them,
but am not one of them. To *read*, you must know how to pronounce
the words without vowels, and with only a sixth-grade Hebrew day
education, I am not that good—besides being lazy and unmotivated.
Instead, I read Torah stories in English when someone else is reciting
them. I started doing this when Josh's dad first became a cantor,
and I found myself in synagogue almost every Saturday. The habit
continued through my son's bar mitzvah and beyond.

The stories about Sarah and Abraham, Isaac, Rebecca, and Jacob
were always my favorites. There is so much jealousy and drama, with
Sarah pining after children so badly she persuades her husband to
sleep with her maid, who is then banished by Sarah. I love how
Rebecca falls off her horse when she sees the man who will become
her husband, and Rachel, with a beauty so profound it persuades

Jacob to work seven years before they can wed, and then another seven years when Rachel's father tricks Jacob into marrying her older sister.

I'm not sure what I think about Jacob's four wives, two of them sisters and two of them the sisters' maids. It was supposed to be about getting children, but if I were Rachel, I would have resisted, children or no. I can understand her attraction to Jacob, though, a man who dared an angel to wrestle and who wouldn't let the angel go without a blessing. I've wanted many times to do something like that myself.

Before I moved to the Midwest, I was living in Park Slope in Brooklyn, in a soon-to-be gentrified neighborhood with a wealthy Reform synagogue, which I did not join. Instead, I found a crumbling synagogue with a painted, faded ceiling. I think the original congregants were a group of older men who must have prayed and read Torah without women participants, because there was a rickety women's balcony that looked like it was on the verge of collapse.

By the time I started going to the synagogue, there was a female rabbi and a group of Park Slope residents like myself, younger men and women trying to figure out new ways of worshipping. Though I never met any of the original people in that congregation—I think they prayed in the basement— I like to think of them at this time of year. They reminded me of my uncle who knew all the prayers by heart and was raised in a time when women didn't participate ritually.

Did Torah make them happy? I don't know, but it mattered to them, and they were passionate about it and about reading it, and that counts for something. A lot. The rabbi *I* got to know at the Brooklyn synagogue was, of course, from a different era. Young, thoughtful, and enthusiastic, she was a seminary graduate and completely comfortable with Torah. We called her Rabbi Julie, and what I liked best about her was how she would ask the congregants questions after her readings, and then, leaning forward, wait patiently for their responses. On Yom Kippur, Rabbi Julie and another female congregant sang the liturgy on the bimah at the front of the synagogue. Their voices seemed to work perfectly together, and it felt like they were singing lullabies weaved into the prayers.

One Shabbat, someone asked me if I had ever had a bat mitzvah, and I explained that the school I attended didn't offer this ritual to girls. I hadn't been trained to read Torah, but was asked to perform a *Galila*, wrapping the Torah scroll before it is put away.

While approaching the Torah to wrap it, people in the aisles smiled at me, and afterwards, they shook my hand and said "*Yasher Koach*," (may your strength be firm). It was the first time I realized I didn't need to be a Hebrew scholar or even devout to be part of a synagogue. That it wasn't about the rabbi or a bat mitzvah, or even wrapping the Torah. It was about being part of our Jewish story.

In Minnesota, I found a shul called Beth Jacob that reminded me of my old synagogue. When there, I listen to people chanting the Torah tropes on holidays and Shabbat. I open the Torah book at my seat and follow along, sometimes in Hebrew but mostly in English. Sometimes I close the book and think up my own stories, which may or may not turn into plays.

I still haven't had a bat mitzvah, mostly because of time, but I'm also not sure I want to stand in front of everyone and read the words aloud in Hebrew anyway. I prefer letting the words lead me up and out to where it all started—or may have started. To Rachel and Jacob, maybe. Egypt and Be'er Sheva, and back again.

What the tropes make me think of has very little to do with Torah law. I know there are people who study it closely in *schools* and universities. I know the Torah codifies a set of rules and that following them is supposed to be the key to a happy life, a "tree of life," as the prayer books say.

But I can't help thinking how the stories *feed* the laws. They tell me there were people living millenniums ago with some of the same struggles I have, and they made the same mistakes. They tell you can wrestle sometimes with an angel, and if you try hard enough, you might—*maybe*—get that angel to bless you. They tell me there are people who can want something so badly—a child, a wife, a blessing—they will risk everything they have to get it.

If you want to know if Torah makes me happy, I couldn't say, exactly. But I can tell you what I think it does make me.

Me.

44

TO COVET OR NOT TO COVET

A FEW DAYS BEFORE Shavuot some years back, I got an intriguing invitation from **Rabbi Zalman** at Chabad, who was putting together a *Tikkun Leil* (special evening service) for the night before the **holiday**. These services typically consist of study sessions that go on late into the evening, and I had wanted to attend one for quite some time. Rabbi Zalman asked me to discuss one of the **Ten Commandments** with the group he was gathering.

To be honest, I hadn't looked at the Commandments in a long while and had completely forgotten about the one that commands us not to covet. Looking at the choices, I thought, *Coveting is something I do, and it's also one of the more subtle commandments.* That made it very dear to my playwright's heart—so that is the one I chose.

> *You shall not covet your neighbor's house; you shall not covet your neighbor's wife, nor his male servant, nor his female servant, nor his ox, nor his donkey, nor anything that is your neighbor's.*

The first thing I thought when reading this text is that *this is a commandment I do not understand.*

I understand not praying to false Gods or even calling on God "in vain," though I'm still not exactly sure why anyone would do that. Maybe to pretend to someone else they were religious when they're not?

Honoring parents, observing Shabbat, not lying or cheating on your spouse or killing—all these make much more sense to me than not coveting. Yet, it made the Big Ten. There must be some reason it's way up there, above so many other things we are commanded to do and not to do.

Isn't coveting something you can accomplish in the privacy of your own home without it bothering anyone or anything else? Is anyone really going to know I'm coveting my neighbor's house, or how she can sleep in when I'm driving to work in the morning?

I try not to be, but I'm covetous of friends' luck sometimes. There are days I want that luck because some of them don't have to work and can devote their lives to art. Sometimes I want their successes.

I guess this makes me a very bad person, or very great sinner—maybe both.

How do you stop coveting, and most of all, why?

I won't say coveting can be motivating, because usually it leaves you stuck in envy and that leads to self-pity more than action on your own behalf. If you're enmeshed in envying someone else, you don't have time to work on your own artistic endeavors, or garden, for that matter. And it's all too easy to find excuses for just about anything if you think, *I'll never have it as good or be as good as this or that person.*

So, coveting often sends you into a spiral that's hard to break. It's obviously bad for you, like smoking, and makes you mentally and emotionally ill. But smoking isn't a fire-alarm quality sin according to the Ten Commandments. Coveting is, and I still don't get it.

It's destructive and even stupid—but why a sin, as in violation of God's law and Torah?

Is it because it can lead to a sin? If you covet someone's wife, would you try and hurt them? I suppose some people have, though I believe it's rare that most of us would do that. Is it because it could lead to stealing your neighbor's stuff?

Is covetousness the root of many of the sins in the Commandments?

I'm not prepared to say yes, but maybe that's because I am not desperate enough to be extremely covetous, and when I'm feeling that way, I tend to do self-destructive things such as over drinking or eating, which makes me feel horrible the next day, of course.

The little things get us started, and what happens then? I suppose *Othello* could tell us, and to me that play has always centered around Iago's famous line. "Beware, my Lord, of jealousy. It is the green-eyed monster which doth mock the meat it feeds on."

Is that what the Commandment is saying? Because if it is, I have to say I like the fact that it's there.

It tells me that someone (One?) was really thinking. *Some One* was saying, "Envy is going to lead to a lot of self-destructive behavior. In one way or another, it could be the root of this list because it can lead to so many branches of it."

So, it gives you another reason not to covet. It lets you know that being happy with what you have isn't just a good idea, it's a requirement to leading a good life. Being grateful for the sun, your marriage, your friends, the abilities, and the talents you have or that were gifted to you are all keys to being happier and more satisfied.

Being commanded not to covet is interesting because it takes the action out of the realm of *options* and puts it squarely into the realm of *requirements*. It says, your own life is important and essential and beautiful, no matter what you have or don't have, no matter what you want that you aren't getting.

You are important. *You* are not an afterthought. *You* are part of a community and who you are matters more than what you have or what you do.

When you forget that, you're sinning against the one God as well as yourself. You are reducing yourself and others to what they have.

I get that you want uninterrupted writing time, and you want your work to be done all over the world and that there are days when you (I) want a completely different life. Whether we get that in this life isn't really up to us. It's up to luck and the ways of the world, and some of it is up to how much we work at it and how much time we have for that work.

It doesn't mean we should stop trying if we don't have enough time to try. It means we should stop comparing ourselves to others, because doing that is the root of all unhappiness, and that unhappiness lasts. And unhappy people can do ugly things—or can easily be led to do them.

Thank you, Rabbi Zalman, for asking me to take this Commandment on. Despite myself, I just may have learned something.

45
NUMBERING MY DAYS

FIRST DAY OF ROSH HASHANAH, Torah service.

I was paging through commentary and my eye floated above a word I don't see often but recognize—*Sheol*. The commentary told me it was the Biblical Jewish term for the *netherworld*, when Jewish people believed in a netherworld.

What is that?

Didn't sound good. *Olam Ha bah* (the world to come) sounds better. Netherworld sounded something like nether regions, and neither seem terrifically hospitable. I do remember reading somewhere that Sheol was considered a place for the weak or weakened ones who, uh, weren't doing too well since they were dead.

The Jewish Encyclopedia cites different sources, but they pretty much come to the same thing; the dead continue "after a fashion" their earthly life (WHAT fashion)? They merely exist without knowledge or feeling; silence reigns and the dead live in an abode of silence.

Does this mean zombies, like in *The Walking Dead*?

I think of all the conversations I've had about what we call the *afterlife,* and how different those conversations are Jewishly when compared to Christian friends, and particularly Catholics. They seemed to have three levels, including Hell, Purgatory (seeming a bit like Sheol), and Heaven.

Of course, Heaven is the most desired spot of these three, although lately it has started to worry me. I tend to think if I awoke after death in a perfect environment with everything I ever wanted and everyone I ever loved or wanted to love I'd—

I don't know. I'd think I was in a coma, or I'd fallen into a diabolical version of *The Good Place.* I would never be able to trust it and I'd be begging whoever was in charge to get me out. The more I think of it, the more I think oblivion is the way to go. Not zombie oblivion, just oblivion.

When I talk about the next world with Jewish friends, clergy, or anyone else who is Jewish and will humor me, I also hear about the possibility that we are dead for a long time and then there is supposed to be a Day of Judgment when the dead rise and some go up to the angels and others go . . . *back to Sheol?* I don't believe there's a Jewish hell, but if Sheol *is* the end, are we just requesting another year of life? I don't know.

It's also hard to explain to Christian friends why I'm so suspicious of heaven. Maybe I've seen *The Matrix* too many times. Or maybe I've just gotten to the point where I have to question why God would wait until you're dead to shower you with everything you ever wanted—or for that matter, punish you.

And if there is such a thing as Christian heaven, what was Jesus doing raising Lazarus from the dead? I'm sure all this sounds flip, but I'm truly not trying to be. I work with older adults, so death is an ever-present guest in my life, often when it's least expected. And as the holidays arrive one by one, Jewish New Year, Yom Kippur, Sukkot, and Simchat Torah, I can't help but think about what we are asking for when we ask to be inscribed in the Book of Life.

Another year of life. Yes. A good life. But what about eternity?

Is it there? Not there? Would it be so bad if it was not?

What about that quote my friend John wrote on the front of my sukkah about numbering your days so you get a heart of wisdom?

If you knew you had forever to live, would you live well? Would you be kind? Ugly? Desperately trying to get noticed? Scared? Gloating? Bored?

Isn't the point of life to number your days so you live and breathe them as intensely and deeply as you can?

The older adults I see on an almost daily basis are teaching me there is no such thing as forever. And I'm not sure, if there is, that I would be much good at going on and on and on. Not to mention the questions I'd have for God and the angels. *All that suffering down here. Yeah, that. Are you noticing?*

Because we really can't (shouldn't) wait to stop all the suffering, and that's what worries me about this notion of afterlife. Is that why the notion isn't usually emphasized much in Jewish tradition?

Looking down at the word Sheol, I still wanted to ask, *What do Jews collectively think about the afterlife?* Should we stop thinking about it altogether? If we believe in it, shouldn't we have a place somewhere that all of us can find out exactly what it means, or is supposed to mean?

Or is life the point and can we just let go of it when it's time, without belaboring and with gratitude for what we've had?

Or does that only work if you've been lucky enough to have the kind of life you'd be grateful for?

I don't know, which is why I'm asking you, I guess. It seems to me the Book of Life is a better image than the After Life. One asks you to do something, and the other asks you to passively absorb it.

Which means I still don't know what to do with this whole notion of an afterlife. I'll stay here a bit longer, I guess. Numbering.

46

BLOOD SPORT

I NEVER EXPECTED to become a boxing fan. I certainly never expected my son to get into boxing, either, though it was likely my fault (isn't it always?), because when he was nine or ten, I brought home a video of *Rocky*.

Josh was hooked immediately and ended up seeing all seven zillion *Rocky* films (or however many there are). When he was in high school, he asked, then begged, then cajoled us into signing him up for boxing lessons.

I had to be convinced not just by Josh, but by his dad, that this was going to be good for him. His father thought it would give Josh more discipline and confidence, plus an outlet for his frustration.

Josh wasn't the kind of kid who loved school—in fact, just the opposite. He was talented, fun-loving, charming, and bright, but sitting in class working on fractions or literature or scientific equations was unappealing.

He liked football but liked boxing more, and in his sophomore year, I let him take a boxing course at the Y, which he looked forward to avidly each week. His teacher was a Golden Gloves winner who had a great rapport with his students, and Josh took to the sport instantly.

I guess I should have known.

Some months later, he was asking, begging, and cajoling me into letting him train with the boxing trainer at a nearby gym. We went back and forth on it for quite a while. I was already wary of the dangers inherent in football, but never having grown up around boys, I knew better than to quibble about it.

I did know more about what repeated blows to the head can do, so tried asking, begging, and cajoling Josh to change his mind, but that wasn't working either. I ended up caving with two conditions:

1. He promised that practice bouts would be fought while he wore a face guard.
2. He promised never to fight with anyone outside of the ring.

The first day, I think the training nearly knocked him sideways, but little by little he got better at it, and little by little I also grew to admire the skill of his trainers and their students.

At night when I picked him up, I would end up having great conversations with Josh's two trainers and began looking forward to them. I learned quite a bit about boxing too.

One of the things I liked best about the trainers was how they insisted that Josh had to get at least a *B* in all his courses, or they wouldn't teach him anymore. They also pushed for higher grades when he got a *B*. I liked how his confidence and discipline grew, just as his father said it would.

Some months after he started boxing, Josh shared one of the reasons he most wanted to learn. "There are just things I haven't told you about school," he said, "but it can be very stressful."

"Yeah, I'm sure," I said, trying to sound just nonchalant enough to make him continue the conversation, as parents do. After a moment, Josh told me what he hadn't revealed before.

"Some kids just say things."

"What things?" I asked.

"You know, like, 'dirty Jew.'"

"Now?"

"Sometimes," he said. "More when I was younger."

The words wounded enough so I was sure he could see the pain on my face. "Oh, honey," I said. I remembered how at his brit ceremony when Josh was an infant, I wanted nothing more than to protect him from the world, but of course no parent can. Was boxing the answer?

"It's not how you're thinking," he said, forcing me to marvel how good he'd become at reading my mind. Boxing didn't fix anything, but somehow knowing how to defend himself made Josh feel stronger inside. He wasn't breaking any promises, he said. But feeling like you can handle yourself if someone comes after you is not a bad thing.

I didn't like the nosebleeds during some of his practice fights or even how he would knock someone down. But after learning about the anti-Semitic remarks he endured at school, I found myself enjoying the fights we saw on TV more, especially the ones with Muhammed Ali, who God knows had faced down his share of hateful words. I had no idea where any of this would land, eventually, but it was certainly an interesting ride, and I'm not sorry I went on it.

Would I recommend boxing for you or your kid? I'd say it was important to know exactly what you're getting into and then figure out if the benefits outweigh the risks or vice versa. My friend Kim grew up in a doctor's family and thinks the risks of blows to the head are too great. I tend to agree with her, but my own experience didn't end up with my son getting many blows, so to me, the risks were manageable.

On the other hand, Josh has shared several stories of people getting memory problems as older adults and those stories are very sobering.

These days, my son is not boxing professionally and pretty much spends most of his time singing. Yet, when he's out walking alone in New York or wherever, I feel kind of better knowing he has some boxing skills.

Besides that, I've gotten to love boxing and would go to see a lot of live fights if I had the time. Being a playwright and growing up in theater taught me the entertainment world is its own kind of blood sport. I think boxing manifests that. And oh, yeah, life. *Isn't that a blood sport, too?*

47

DYBBUKS, GOLEMS, AND THE POSSESSION: A NEW LOOK AT JEWISH EXORCISM

IT WAS AN AWFUL DAY, and I was in no mood for listening. But when I said, "Things couldn't be worse," I was jogged out of my rant by a friend who started screaming at me. "Don't say that!" she yelled so loudly that I looked at her, surprised. "I mean, hey," she continued more calmly. "Things can *always* be worse."

Maybe that's why I love horror movies and have since I was a child. It could be because my father loved them and used to entertain me by pretending to be *The Phantom of the Opera*. Or maybe it's because no matter what I'm going through, people in horror movies always have it so much worse. And they can scream about it, too.

In *The Exorcist*—one of my favorite movies—the most telling scene to me is the one where the demon/little girl's head turns languidly toward Father Karras.

"It's a perfect day for an exorcism," the demon says, and when asked why, he says, "It will bring us together."

"You and Regan?" the priest asks.

"You and me."

For my money, that's the money quote. Because the fact that demons are chasing people who want to be close to God most interests me about demons. There's also something interesting about people being willing to try to exorcise demons, though it wasn't until I saw the film *The Possession* that I started thinking about Jewish exorcism. Like most of us, I tend to think of the ritual as a Catholic thing. But *The Possession* made me realize it's more likely to be something that began with rabbis, instead.

One of the first mentions of exorcism in the Bible alludes to an evil spirit affecting King Saul, which is driven out by David's music. Digging around a bit more, I found a Biblical story about the angel Raphael teaching someone named Tobit how to ban evil spirits. And Josephus—a Jewish-turned-Roman historian with an amazing talent for putting readers to sleep—wrote something about a man named Eleazar "releasing people that were demonical."

As a child, I remember seeing a movie that appeared to be a Jewish exorcism, with men blowing the Ram's horns used on the New Year to exorcise evil spirits, then reading the play *The Dybbuk*, which I very much liked, and then a story by Cynthia Ozick about a clay creature that I still count as a great favorite. An Isaac Bashevis Singer story about warring Hasidic sects fighting over the best way to exorcise a young woman's demon is the first and only possession tale I've seen with a sense of humor. (Yet another reason to love Isaac B.)

But what's the Jewish position on exorcism now? Mainstream Judaism frowns on mysticism and spiritualism, which are seen as dangerous influences on religious faith. Then again, what about those chicken rituals on Yom Kippur? I haven't talked about them here because when *I* think about them, our roots seem to me at least a little bit breathless. And the chicken rituals aren't the only *oddities*, to use a charitable word.

Cynthia Ozick's story is a reimagining of the legend about the

Golem of Prague, a clay figure constructed by Rabbi Judah Loew ben Bezalel. He brought it to life through rituals and prayers to protect Jews from anti-Semitic attacks throughout history. Over time, the golem became more violent, and the rabbi was unable to control his creation. I thought of this while watching *The Possession* because it's sort of a Jewish take on *The Exorcist*.

The Possession follows the story of a little girl whose father buys her a box covered with Hebrew letters. The box turns out to have a *dybbuk* (disembodied spirit) that consumes children. Once the little girl opens the box, the dybbuk begins to inhabit her. There are some great moments here, notably when the little girl looks in a mirror (I won't tell but check out the trailer), and seeing the rapper Matisyahu as a fledgling exorcist offers a great peek into what could be a most exceptional profession. Yet I couldn't help thinking that while so much in this film seemed to echo *The Exorcist*, there wasn't much that went beyond it. Still, that didn't stop me from enjoying the film.

I loved how the box in *The Possession* held a mirror so the dybbuk would have to see itself for eternity, knowing it had turned away from God. I loved how they had to call it by name to subdue it and had to find the name. This made me think of the ancient Jewish priests, calling out God's name before we lost it.

"How on earth did you lose the name of God?" my friend John once asked. I could only clomp my hand to my forehead and say, "Who knows?"

The movie also made me realize I am still intrigued by the idea of dybbuks, golems, and Jewish exorcism. I think we Jews may be uncomfortable with these things because we already have enough trouble with seeming *different* in the wider world. Maybe that's why we were all too glad to let Catholics take over, in public perception at least, via movies like *The Exorcist*.

Mainly, I think seeing *The Possession* got me excited about the idea that we may be willing to surface with some of our own dybbuk stories again. Because what the Jews know, and know well, is that horror movies can be all too real sometimes.

And whether or not you have a dybbuk inside you, make no mistake.

It can *always* be worse.

48
THOSE WHO WAIT

FOR THE FIRST YEAR of my son's life, I was done wanting to be an award-winning playwright or write novels or musicals. All I wanted was to sleep.

I did not succeed, and it comes as no surprise that I have raised an insomniac. That boy wore me out, I'm here to tell you. As an infant, he stayed up past midnight and woke at three. Sometimes he was hungry, but most often he simply wanted to play.

Somehow or other, we both survived those early months and little by little, I got him closer to a reasonable bedtime. By reasonable I mean 10 p.m., graduating to 9 p.m. on school nights, and yes, I tried for 8:30 p.m. Where he gets his energy from, God only knows. (Actually, I *do* know. It's his dad.)

I myself have a fairly sluggish disposition, meaning give me a bed and ten times out of ten, I'll want to sleep in it. I did become awake enough to turn into a playwright and write some middle-grade/YA books. But only just.

Which is why, when parents tell me their kids go to bed at 7 or 7:30 p.m., I want to melt down just like a two-year-old. I have never known that child and I never, ever will. Not for me the long evenings on the veranda, sipping wine or mint juleps or whatever parents sip when their kids go to bed early and they have more than seven minutes to themselves.

On the other hand, I did become a consummate expert at bribery, thinking up all sorts of imaginative ways to entice my son into his bed. One included singing the Shema prayer traditionally said at bedtime. After the first line which says, "Hear O Israel, the Lord Our God, the Lord is One," we sang the second verse together. The melody usually put me to sleep and got him more wound up, so we had to do it three or four times until I gave up and begged him just to *try* sleeping. Sometimes, he took pity on me and agreed.

Mostly, though, he would sleep for a couple of hours and then want to come into his parents' bedroom to chat. I finally gave in and placed a mat next to my bed, on the condition that he would go to sleep—or at least act like it.

I am certainly a believer in flashlights and board books that can slip under the covers, though my husband, Pete, would tell you he is not. But the entertainment of certain books or comics can be a perfect way to keep your kid quiet, I promise you.

Of course, the experts who write books about this stuff said we were raising a kid who will never figure out how to sleep alone. "Phooey," I say. Do *you* want to sleep alone? Weren't cats invented for the very purpose of making sure we don't have to?

Now my son is older, and I know he still has a lot of trouble sleeping. I believe it is because he has an adventurer's mind and a performer's heart, and the soundtrack pulses through him like jazz, making it hard to find the serenity needed to enter a sleeper's wonderland.

I tell him about meditation and milk and soft music, but I know none of it is helping. I tell him to try the Shema, but he reminds me that never worked in the first place. I tell him wait until he has a kid, and then he'll start sleeping like the babies everyone else talks about who nod off in their mother's arms at a moment's notice.

I *don't* tell him his kid won't let him nod off. But I smile, just a little, because we're on the phone and he can't see me. I hope I get to meet this kid.

Good things come to those who wait.

49

GODLY BEATS

DEPENDING ON WHO YOU ARE and where you live, you're likely to agree we're going through terrifying times. I've been told every generation feels that way, but I think we have special reason to think so, since a viral pandemic known as COVID-19 decided to attack us. I've been trying to escape into writing part three of my Beat Street Series for middle-grade and YA readers, along with this book.

Set in Greenwich Village, Washington, DC, and San Francisco in 1958, the series is about a young girl growing up amid Beat Generation artists and poets who wants to be a poet herself. I began this series for many reasons. One, I was attracted to the freedom and rebellion of Beat culture, which I think was inherited by artists in the 1960s like Patty Smith and Robert Mapplethorpe and Leonard Cohen whose song "Bird on a Wire" resonates with me. But the main reason I started writing about Beats was my attraction to Jack Kerouac's passion for his own faith and how that informed him as a writer.

Of course, most Beats were not known for being religious, and there is no religious content in the Beat Street books. I've heard people say a lot of famous Beats were Jewish; I have found no evidence of it, though. Yes, Allen Ginsberg was probably the most famous Jewish Beat poet. I also love the poetry of Elise Cowan, who had a relationship with Ginsberg, though his lifelong love was poet Peter Orlovsky. Bob Kaufman said he was the son a German-Jewish father and a Roman Catholic African-American mother from Martinique.

What I find interesting about the Beats is that none of them would tell you he or she was religious, but they all shared a religious dedication to art. Some years ago, I was working in an acting company called Time and Space Limited. The director said it was no accident we had all come from religious backgrounds, because art requires the same kind of attention and dedication as religion does.

I think she was right.

Did Jack Kerouac's Catholic roots inform so much of his writing? According to Kerouac, *On the Road* "was really a story about two Catholic buddies roaming the country in search of God. And we found Him," he writes, explaining how God was in the San Francisco sky and in his friend "sweating out of his forehead."

I love that he did and didn't want to speak about God. But in a very real sense, Kerouac dedicated his life in the same way a monk does, and I think all his offerings were meant first for God.

Allen Ginsberg, meanwhile, may not have grown up in a religious home, but his father was a published poet, and if you spend any time reading the younger Ginsberg's work, you can see more than spiritual threads in it; you can also see Jewish roots. One of Ginsberg's most famous poems, called "Kaddish" (like the mourner's prayer), was written in memory of his mother Naomi.

Ginsberg talks about reading the Kaddish prayer aloud and how it made him weep. His story about his mother's struggles with mental illness are heartbreaking and stunning, wrapped perfectly around the Kaddish prayer that he or others in his family may have said for her.

I could go on, teasing out more Jewish poets or exploring the Jewish-Buddhist connection in Beats—though it was Kerouac, after all, who wrote *Dharma Bums*. But what interests me most is the idea of dedication and religion, and how they both seem to make a perfect storm—for art.

I'm not at all sure that's what my main character Ruby Tabeata would tell you in *The Beat on Ruby's Street*. I do think she has that same dedication in her spirit, though, whether she knows where it comes from or not. I *can* tell you that my own Jewish background helped give me the discipline and dedication I needed to become a playwright, and to write altogether. Whether it has something to do with the holidays (derived from the words *holy* and *day*), prayers, the beauty and strangeness of Hebrew letters and prayers, or all the above, I can't exactly say; but all of these combined in me to feed the creativity I have and hope to have.

Like Kerouac's buddies, I too am in search of God. But if you asked me to check off the ways I find God—through rituals, writing, holidays, relationships, shul, or something more—I'd have to say that I don't know. All of the above?

50
COMING-OUT RABBI

DOES THE THOUGHT of High Holy Day services make you want to scurry into bed and pull the covers over your nose? Does the thought of any synagogue service do the same?

We don't want to admit it—at least I don't—but even rabbis will sometimes acknowledge that services can be boring. I say this as a woman once married to a cantor and whose son became one too, which means I've been to a lot of services. So, when a friend who moved to DC wrote me about a Kol Nidrei Day of Atonement service at a Conservative synagogue called Adas Israel that was "amazing," I had doubts.

What was so amazing about it, I asked? His answer came in five paragraphs, and by the end, I wanted nothing more than to join him. He started by saying the service was outside, under the stars, which may be easier in DC than Minnesota.

The synagogue had engaged Israeli folk singers and musicians who played, chanted, and sang the liturgy, using instruments from ancient times. The service was set up as a sing-along so the congregation could participate in almost everything. My friend described it as a Jewish version of singing along with Handel's Messiah.

The Israeli and Sephardic melodies brought new energy to the prayers, my friend said, and engaged him much more than the classic Ashkenazy melodies he'd grown up singing. At that point, a famous cellist performed what my friend called a "phenomenally moving rendition" of the service's opening prayer, which was then chanted and sung by everyone with the cantor and folk choir.

Reading this, I thought even if a synagogue was Orthodox and didn't want to use instruments, the chants and communal singing outdoors would also be exceptional. And I wanted to see more of this shul.

"Being under the stars with a big moon lighting our prayer books was an extraordinary experience by itself," my friend added.

I'm telling you this because the service really intrigued me, though it seemed *The Washington Post* and nearly every other major mainstream newspaper were much more interested in the synagogue rabbi's personal life than the experience he offers to congregants.

What did the articles say? The rabbi had recently come out as a gay man. He and his wife, who seem very close and loving according to the article my friend shared, were getting ready to separate so the rabbi could move forward with his new life. *The Washington Post* headline described what most papers were saying. *In a DC rabbi's e-mail, revelation and relief: 'I am a gay man.'*

First, second, and third, I support the rabbi's choice and feel for him and his wife. I think they must both be extraordinary people. I remember the days when rabbis and cantors always had to be male, and when being gay or a woman disqualified you from leading a service. I remember a brilliant, talented, compassionate woman rabbi who came out and was promptly fired, and other women and men who struggled to find their place as clergy and were denied. Seeing them on pulpits now, and seeing how much they add to our services, makes me furious that whoever was in charge disrespected them and kept them from their chosen professions.

But here's what I don't understand. Why isn't anyone reporting on the service this particular rabbi created? Why is it that one of the most interesting services in the country isn't noticed by reporters and is sloughed off in favor of a rabbi's private life?

Huffpo, Washpo . . . et al, I understand that you want us to know that more and more clergy are coming out and that our synagogues are better for it. Yet if there are stories about High Holy Day services that make us sit up and take notice, I'm not seeing them, because you're not covering them. Ever.

My friend continued his description of the service and all I could do was imagine the scene he created. "No sermon. No requests for donations. No administrative announcements. Just the liturgy as roadmap, HaShem's sky, the officiants, and the congregation seeking repentance and atonement together. A community of Jews communing together. There was a spirituality present that I had not sensed before, brought about by the milieu. As we prayed and sang, pedestrians gathered on the streets surrounding the shul's plaza and watched and listened to the service."

My friend concluded by saying it was a glorious way to begin the new year.

While the *Post* let me know the rabbi's name, age, and email to the congregation detailing his decision to come out, I learned nothing about the experiences people were enjoying at his synagogue. Would they describe Nobel winner Malala Yousafzai by talking about her private life?

In less than a week, the High Holy Day season will end, and readers will likely forget about this story. But I have a feeling the people who attended services at Adas will not forget what they saw and heard there. What I'm praying for, this New Year, is that the time comes (speedily, yeah, and soon) when we open the paper and read about what rabbis are doing in their congregations instead of in their marriages. Because I'd like very much to follow their examples to find new energy and meaning in the most ancient ceremonies and practice.

51

IN 2005, an illness brought my father to the hospital. He was ninety and was beginning, in his way, to rehearse us for his death. It was easy to imagine in a far-off way, but not in this hospital room, with the hieroglyphs of a heart monitor etching green in my face.

A week later he was better, and I could breathe, push it away again. The Jewish New Year was beginning, and the Ten Days of Awe. But I couldn't think of Judgment or sin.

I walked the streets as the light fades, thinking, *Heaven. I'm not sure. I am afraid to believe in it, thinking it can't be what most of us believe.*

I didn't say this joyfully or think of it with joy. Rather, it was like being in the dark, living with a cloud over the eyes, a veil on the face. Not believing in life after death means there is nothing on the horizon; it is only real life. No magic. Nothing moves.

So again, I thought, *Heaven*, but my rational mind hushed it out like a candle. It took a walk to tease it out again, like a story, on a night in October too warm to be believable, and yet it was, and there I was, in the light of a streetlamp.

Thinking, *If I did believe, what would I see?*

Something like this night, with the sun going down and the tops of branches fanning sky in the Upper Midwest. Everything is beautiful, and fragile, as you start upward, flying away from leaves falling soundlessly and men holding children's hands as they walk their dogs.

Higher and faster, you are leaping over streets and fields and woods. Not flying the way birds do. It is like flying in dreams. At one point in my twenties, I started having strange flying dreams where I seemed to jump out of my body and move through the sky so rapidly it terrified me, and I had to slow down. It was the strongest sensation I ever had of what it must be like to be a bird. I have no idea where this dream came from, and missed it terribly when it stopped, but I've never been able to dream it again.

This must be, I thought, *what ascending would be like after a death*. Fast, faster, fastest, flying everywhere, and you don't miss the world below. You will later miss the love you shared in a house with a man and child and your friends and relatives, but for now you are floating freely, and there is a freedom in your heart you never felt because you can go anywhere, anywhere at all.

All the things you wanted and never found. All the people you wanted to see—who could not see you, the songs, lovers, glory, beauty you never had—are gone, and so your pain is gone, because your wanting is over. Instead is only flight, and what is possible.

At the end is a house, on the edge of a field, under oak trees. It's still warm as you walk outside, with the screen door slamming behind you. All the love you found in your first love, all the love you knew how to give in your second, is at the end of the roadway. Folds you in its arms and you can rest there until morning.

Then again. Taking flight.

52
LAST DANCE

MEMORY: I AM LIGHTING MENORAH CANDLES at Hanukkah and my father isn't home yet. My mother is behind me, and as I light each candle, we say blessings together. A plateful of potato *latkes* (pancakes) waits on the table. I am trying to time the blessings with my father's arrival because I want to dance on his shoes. I am seven years old.

Mom tries calling my father at his store. "Tony? This is Faye. Has Max left yet?" He has, but only fifteen minutes ago because December is a busy time in retail. So, our little dance will have to wait.

We did a lot of dancing when I was small. Once the Hanukkah candles were lit, we sang all the songs and danced like magpies while my mother finished cooking. When my dad was late, my mom and I sat down to eat once the lighting was done. But when my father arrived, he did not fail me. We sang "Hanukkah, Oh Hanukkah" and half a dozen other songs. It seemed he would never tire of dancing me around.

Years later, we were at Emerald Crest, a small assisted-living community specializing in Alzheimer's and similar conditions. My husband and son and I saw my father several times a week, taking him out for bagels and tea. But he knew he wasn't at home and desperately wanted to be. If the doctors hadn't told us he couldn't live on his own anymore, I wouldn't have brought him out here. At the same time, I'm glad we did.

I loved having my dad around. He was fun and funny, with twinkly blue eyes and a megawatt smile. Nurses and aides were in love with him, and visitors always trotted over to joke with my dad. On warm days, we sat outside by a pond watching geese hunt for crumbs. "A penny for your thoughts," he always said.

My dad, Max, grew up in Bayonne, New Jersey, at the height of the Depression. He recalled trolling the streets for food with his twin brother, Harry. At nineteen my father was rescued by President Roosevelt, who instituted the Civilian Conservation Corps in rural areas. Max went to Idaho, and throughout his life he talked about the beautiful tall pines framing his campgrounds.

Some years later, he met my mother. They married a month before he was shipped off to boot camp and then the Philippines, where he was stationed during World War II. "Are you sure you want to marry me?" he had asked. "I could lose an arm or a leg—or not come back at all."

"I'll take my chances," my mother is reported to have said. She passed away in 2000, leaving him to weep in their king-size bed on nights that may have seemed unlikely to end. The hardest thing I ever did—even harder than leaving my little boy on his first day of kindergarten—was leaving my dad alone in New Jersey when I had to return home after my mother's funeral. When he moved to Minnesota, it was a relief to know I could leave work and see him within twenty minutes—maybe for both of us.

The evening I am thinking of now began when it was just past four and the sky was already darkening. It was the first of eight nights of Hanukkah, and we were in a room full of older adults with various conditions—the most obvious one being loneliness. One woman said of her relatives, "I think they're afraid of old age. Afraid they'll catch it."

She may be right. In the short time I saw my father's health decline, I had learned much about how we view older adults. I am not talking about staff members—I am talking about the rest of us. But I have learned; I am still learning.

During the last year or so of his life, my father lost some of his ability to verbalize, but retained his sense of humor and warmth. We could hold hands on the couch for hours and understand each other perfectly. And if something was wrong and I needed to talk about it, I knew I could—and my dad would listen.

I knew that because whatever I know of gentleness, kindness, and grace, I learned from my father. Yet the Alzheimer's often felt like it was keeping us apart.

By the year 2050, Minnesota's cases of Alzheimer's are expected to reach 200,000, according to a study at the Alzheimer's Association. Those who have it may be us. I would like us to see them, though we mostly ignore them. I would like us to see them differently. Maybe Hanukkah is a good way to start.

I've tried to emphasize in these pages that it's not a major holiday like Christmas, but Hanukkah has its own spark. I think it was meant to be mostly about defiance, particularly the defiance of Jews who refused to give up their traditions, even when it would have been prudent to do so. No matter what condition we are in, we are still part of a community that has lit candles on Hanukkah for thousands of years. And each one of us still has some Hanukkah light in our eyes.

The night I was with my dad at Emerald Crest, staff asked me to share the holiday candle-lighting ceremony. On the first night, I told them, you light only one candle using a shammash-caretaker candle. I sang the blessings, and my father recognized them immediately. When I looked at him, he flashed a broad smile.

When the blessings were finished, I took my father's hand while reaching for the woman next to me. I asked people to dance around the menorah and began to sing. Seeing this, a staffer took someone else's hand, and in a few seconds, everyone was dancing. I stole a glance at my father. The light of the candles was reflected in his face.

Like others in this room, my father may have given an *impression* of frailty. But, in fact, he was not. He walked every day and sometimes shared memories of World War II, his marriage, and his years as a storekeeper. He had always been a fine storyteller, with an eye for telling details. When recalling his first night in the Army, he used to joke about finding a cockroach while draining his coffee mug. "I threw it out and finished drinking," he said, with a wink.

Dancing with my father, I wanted to believe some things are eternal, whether there's life after death or not. Driving home, I couldn't help but think of the little girl whose father danced her around the menorah, knowing if I asked, my dad would again invite me to jump on his shoes.

I think of it now, years after his death, still seeing my father's eyes in the flames of Hanukkah. Tonight, I have only a picture that does little justice to him, but it will have to do.

Maybe somewhere, we are still dancing together. In the light.

53
WHO NEEDS A MINYAN?

FOR THE PAST TWO WEEKS, Amy's life has been a mess. Since her grandfather died, she has been scrambling to run his movie-rental business, which hasn't been going well since people started using Netflix. Her partner suggests porn—they are, after all, in a college town—and her best friend thinks she's not jazzing up the store enough. But Amy's main problem is finding a way to say goodbye to her grandfather.

The main thing driving Amy these days is saying the Kaddish prayer for her grandfather, but finding friends or neighbors to help her do it is almost impossible. She could join a synagogue, but she doesn't really feel connected and doesn't even know what she believes in a Jewish sense.

Amy is me—and of course, not me. She is a character I created in a play called *If You Don't Weaken*. When my father died some years ago, I tried to say Kaddish every day, but found it hard to get to my synagogue before work in the morning. Instead, I went to another shul's evening service, which was populated by older people and often struggling to find a *minyan*, or quorum of ten. That's the minimum number needed to make a minyan, which is needed to say the Kaddish prayer.

If you had only to say it once, Kaddish would be easy. But to fulfill your obligation to the deceased, the prayer has to be recited every day for a year. The older people in the decrepit shul Amy attends explain that her grandfather's soul will hover round her for the coming year to be sure she is all right; if she doesn't keep saying Kaddish, her grandfather cannot move on.

I'm not sure where I heard this, but on days when I wanted to say Kaddish and we waited in vain for people to show up, I couldn't help but wonder if it was true. As a child I heard stories about people going outside of their shuls and beating the bushes for a minyan, but never really understood why you needed one to pray. I still don't, but like so many things in Jewish life, we seem to have no choice but to follow these laws.

I struggle with rules and laws, and often try to find the *want* inside them instead of the *need*. It's likely because I am a rebellious soul who has trouble with authority, and what else is God but the Ultimate Authority? Or it may be that I've never been able to control my curiosity, which is why I started writing, which, of course, gave me the perfect excuse to explore things like this.

The word *minyan* is rooted in Hebrew and means to count or number. According to the Jerusalem Talmud, the requirement of a ten-person minyan comes from the combination of two Biblical words and verses. The first one is the word *congregation* in a commandment to be holy.

There's also another reference to the ten sons of the Biblical patriarch Jacob who traveled to Egypt to find food during a famine. Well, now we may be getting somewhere. Then again, I am not one of those *have-to* persons. I prefer to look for why they might have *wanted* to insist on ten people and go from there.

What Amy finds—and what I found—is the minyan brings you to the same place every day, at the same time, so you can have a place to express, or at least get your arms around, saying goodbye to someone you love. Before and after you say the prayer, sometimes years after, you may have days when you want to say, *I miss you. I can't even bear it here without you.*

But there is no one you can really talk to about that, because, as we all know, death is inevitable and final—unless you are one of the lucky people who have no doubts about God and an afterlife. Perhaps the Kaddish prayer, which doesn't mention the word death and instead talks only of what is eternal, is a way to get *us* to move on, more than the people we are mourning.

At the same time, there is always a part of us that won't and can't. My father's voice, smile, spark, and spirit have informed the way I live and love others. He never went to a minyan, and at one point he told me he thought religion was a fairy tale and didn't believe in God. Yet, I think if someone had asked him to join a minyan to help someone else, he would have. When I am miserable or anxious, I find myself talking to him and sometimes asking him for help; I don't want to think about whether he can really hear me.

Even still, the act of going to a minyan—for yourself or for others—helps us call out to that presence, aloud. So, the idea of at least ten people could be more than a rule here. It could be there to make sure you are feeling less alone.

I'm pretty sure Amy is going to discover that. She asks a pole dancer, Talmud Torah students, her African American mail carrier who was adopted by Jewish parents, a lawyer in her neighborhood, and a woman in the park who brings her dog. All of them join Amy and the older adults she befriends at a dark and crumbling shul to say the Kaddish. I just hope they stay long enough to help her through.

54
WOLF CIRCLE HEALING

I WOKE UP THINKING about the grandparents I always wanted to know and never met. As a child, I begged for grandparent stories, since all four of mine had died before I was born. My parents obliged with the usual stories—my grandmother's gentleness and love for Charlie Chaplain movies and my grandfather's colorful life and music—but there were also darker nightmare tales born of the woods of Eastern Europe.

What I'm talking about here are wolves. Bridal parties. And wolves, eating same. Did you ever hear those stories? They snaked into my childhood dreams and gave me a lifelong fear of traveling by sleigh through the snow at night. Which is a shame, because if you live in the Midwest, there are some very tempting possibilities for winter sleigh rides.

The stories I heard were stories my parents heard as children. My grandparents came to this country in the late 1800s, and illnesses took them, not wolves. I don't know who told these stories or why or when; I just know the main trope was one of a bride and groom in a sleigh weighted down with alcohol and delicacies. Their sleigh may have broken, or they may have been derailed by bandits. I don't know. But after they were left alone, the wolves began to circle them and—you can guess the rest.

I had an inkling of this last fall, on a county road about a mile from home. There were cars behind me but nothing ahead, and I was trying to keep up my speed at thirty-five miles an hour. In the space of a millisecond, a huge buck with antlers at least two feet long from end to end bolted out in front of me, crossing the road. There was no time to think; I hit the brakes as hard as I could.

Because there was no snow on the ground, I didn't slide into a tree or him or anywhere else, and the buck leapt across the road in a few seconds. The cars behind me didn't even see him and were honking because I stopped. It seemed a kind of miracle, and as I drove on, I said the Great Miracle prayer.

I could not talk to the deer and tell it to stop dashing out into crossings. There is no possibility of reasoning with an animal, a baby, or a virus. Thinking of it now, months later, I can only wonder if we have indeed become the bridal party my parents spoke of, surrounded by wolves.

In 2020, the COVID-19 pandemic began overseas. It spread throughout Europe and the Western US—and then began to reach pandemic proportions here. The disease rolled in slowly but persistently, like a dark fog in a horror movie. Suddenly, the world we knew, which I took for granted, had to slam on the brakes to keep from imploding.

Restaurants, bars, theaters, stores, and schools had to close, and gatherings of more than ten were forbidden indoors. A massive number of people were out of work, including artists and writers.

We also had to start wearing masks to stop the spread, and while most people (including me) felt this was necessary, it became politicized to the point where people shot clerks who tried to enforce rules about wearing masks before you came into their stores.

How did we get here? I know pundits and historians will ponder that question and eventually share it with us. At the time of this writing, I can only share what was happening to me and others I know.

Josh was working at his first job as a cantor, leading services through song and prayer at a synagogue. I was supposed to visit him during Passover, but those plans were scuttled when everyone figured out the disease is spread by droplets when we talk, sing, cough, or sneeze. Sitting close to another person on a plane just felt too risky.

It was a year of waking up hoping the world will right itself, while the trajectory seemed determined to go exactly the opposite of righting. Pete and I sometimes laughed, thinking the worst thing that could have happened to us this past year was the mice trying to enter our basement. Then (drumroll please) came the Zombie Apocalypse, with a dead virus wrapped in a living sleeve that doggedly, persistently, and seemingly endlessly seeks out hosts.

In May, the world erupted yet again when a Black man named George Floyd was murdered by police in Minneapolis. His name is added to a long list of deaths caused by entrenched racism and widespread indifference. Protests began here and then worldwide, and though they gave me hope some days the system had a chance of changing, other days we seemed stuck in a loop without the possibility of hope.

The more we saw around us that month, the clearer it became; COVID-19 wasn't the only virus that needed healing. If only we tried as hard at solving racism as we did with fixing the virus, wouldn't we have done better by now? Instead, the president sent troops to arrest peaceful protesters.

Around this time, my husband came down with shingles in his eye and had to have three surgeries in as many months, which sent us rushing to doctors and terrified about vision loss. Then a friend and coworker died from COVID, and at that point, I started struggling with serious depression, willing myself to keep from shutting down.

I wanted badly to go back to a moment when I'd never even heard of COVID-19. Failing that, I wanted to return to a time when I believed the heinous virus we were living through would be brief, or at least briefer. That little window of time would have been in March, a few days before our governor's orders to stay home. I had a feeling the orders were coming. I wanted to buy a dress for my son's wedding, then scheduled for August, and asked my husband to go with me.

We settled on a department store near home. I didn't realize it then, but it was one of the last times I would talk to strangers for a while, without social distancing rules that keep us at least six feet apart—and without wearing masks. I spoke with a woman and her daughter shopping for a prom dress, and they recommended a couple of dresses for me.

The salesperson was so relaxed and serene, I began to feel that way, too. She invited me into the changing room, which was at least as big as my kitchen, and told my husband he could go in with me. We were pretty much alone, as there were hardly any people in the store after the mother and daughter went home. A piano recording played throughout our visit, and I began to feel as though there was no pandemic or illness or anything that would hurt me or anyone I knew.

For the next hour, I texted pictures of the dresses I tried on to my son's fiancé. We all finally settled on a navy-blue gown that made me feel like I was in a painting. Someone came in to show me shoes, and someone else came to take the dress in a bit. We had arrived at seven and left at nine; I have never, ever spent that much time in a store looking for one dress—even my own wedding dress.

To be honest, if the store had still been open, I wouldn't have left. I didn't want to go home. I didn't want to return to *normal* life, knowing it wasn't at all normal and might not be for a very long time. I wanted to believe I would be wearing that dress very soon.

Of course, I didn't see my son for many months, and I cried much more than I want to admit. I'd also burst out laughing periodically, thinking, who would believe this if they're reading it years from now? Won't they think I made it up? Meanwhile, the blue dress hung in the closet, like something in the fractured fairy tale cartoons I devoured as a child.

Then came a day when Josh invited me to a virtual Shabbat service at his synagogue. I watched him put his mask on to read Torah and take it off again when he walked far away enough from congregants to sing to them. I could see the respect and care with which my son and others running the service treated the prayers and those of us listening. When Josh started singing the prayer for healing, he used the Debbie Friedman composition, and I stood to sing it with him.

The prayer's title *Mi Shebeirach* comes from the two first words of the prayer, which is common in the liturgy.

Mi shebeirach avoteinu
M'kor hab'racha l'imoteinu
May the source of strength,
Who blessed the ones before us,
Help us find the courage to make our lives a blessing,
And let us say, Amen.
Mi shebeirach imoteinu
M'kor habrachah l'avoteinu
Bless those in need of healing with refuah shlemah
The renewal of body, the renewal of spirit
And let us say, Amen.

Watching the congregation sing this prayer made me feel that at least some measure of hope remained. In my synagogue, the tradition is that each person with a loved one who is ill stands up after the Torah service. The rabbi then points to each congregant, who says their loved one's name. Just saying someone's name, I think, brings them into your life in ways it might not otherwise.

Sarah. Jake. Mikaela. Sharon. David. Robert. Seth.

We are calling on you, HaShem, to heal those of us who have fallen ill, and there are many. We are calling on You to have mercy on those who are suffering and scared and alone.

We are calling on You and saying their names.

Their names are our own.

We are calling on You as a community. Wolves are circling and we need to get away.

We are standing together all over the world, in the present moment. We are here because we want to heal.

Because we need to heal.

We will do whatever we can to bring about this healing, physically and mentally. What I can do now begins with Mi Shebeirach. Every other community will begin with a different ritual, but all of them tell us the same thing.

Healing is possible.

We are saying each other's names so you will know which one of us is in need of You.

We are saying each other's names so we ourselves will know each other.

Perhaps that's what matters now. What You wanted us to do.

55

BIG LITTLE THING

WE WERE APPROACHING September when my son's fiancé, Jamie, sent me a Zoom invitation to a wedding shower. The wedding was still on the table, though postponed for a while, so on the appointed day, my husband Pete and I logged on to our computers and waited with other relatives.

We saw the summer-green lawn of a friend's home in New Jersey. A few tables were situated near a food table, which looked suspiciously fancy, but I wasn't tracking. We said hello to Jamie's sister, Emily, her husband, Isaac, and their little one, Ruthie. Jamie's parents were watching by Zoom like we were.

We talked and waited for what seemed like hours, though it was probably only forty-five minutes. We kept hearing updates about the couple "in traffic" or "on their way." Then suddenly, Jamie and Josh appeared on our screens—he in an elegant gray suit and Jamie in . . . *what?* A wedding dress?

Pete looked over at me. "I think this is a real wedding," he said. My mouth dropped open; no sound came out—and for the next twenty minutes, Emily officiated. She had gotten some sort of online credential and was therefore legally able to marry her sister to my son.

Emily began with a story of Josh arranging to meet Jamie. When he asked her out, she cautioned, "You know if we meet, you're going to fall in love with me." Josh didn't say he'd take his chances, but that's what I imagined he'd said. While Emily talked, we watched Josh and Jamie face each other as guests sat in socially distanced positions on the lawn. We watched them laughing, and we laughed with them. And though I desperately wanted to be there, I was unimaginably grateful they had decided to move ahead with their joy.

As the ceremony ended, Emily thanked the powers vested in her by the state of New Jersey . . . "and all those years of seminary school," she said. We laughed again and applauded the bride and groom.

Some days later, Jamie texted me that the Jewish ceremony would be rescheduled for 2021. I can tell you that it happened, and Jamie circled Josh seven times while the cantor chanted seven blessings. As the ceremony ended, Josh wrapped a glass in a napkin and broke it underfoot, symbolizing either the destruction of the Temple in long-ago Jerusalem or the fact that there is still oppression in the world. Others say the glass breaking is to remember that marriage offers sorrow as well as happiness, and reminds us to stand by each other when times are hard.

It was an extraordinarily beautiful celebration—and yes, I wore the blue dress. But I suspect the first ceremony, with its sun-dappled yard and sly glances between bride and groom, will always be the one I like best. It was goofy and brilliant and a little subversive, like an exploding fire hydrant on a scorching afternoon.

At this point, vaccines and medications have made a lot of difference, and though the disease keeps mutating, it is not half so deadly as it was. But my path to healing didn't start with vaccines. It started in the backyard of Josh and Jamie's friends, heading straight for the mouth of that big-little word hope.

I started this book with a divorce, so I suppose it's only fitting to end with a wedding. I guess that means you can accuse me of being an impossible romantic. I can only say in my defense, my ending wasn't planned. Like you, I was led here. By the story, by the holidays, by a year of crooked lines, and by two young voices who insisted they could steer us in the dark. I agreed to follow them because I wanted to go where they were going. And because everything I've told you is the only way I know to go.

ACKNOWLEDGMENTS

MY FIRST DEBT goes to Leora Maccabee, founder of *TC Jewfolk*. Thank you, Leora, for asking me to write about the Jewish side of my journey and cheering me on when I did. I also want to thank former Managing Editor Emily Cornell for her imaginative reactions to my stories; and Editor/Director of Communications Lonny Goldsmith and Executive Director Libby Goldstein Parker for their encouragement and support.

As every writer knows, books reach their best audiences through publishers that believe in them. I want to thank John Koehler at Koehler Books for his passion for the printed word and sense of humor; and Joe Coccaro for his patient and thoughtful editing, which includes asking the right questions and making sure I answered them. I also want to thank Skyler Kratofil for her beautiful cover and book design, and Miranda Dillon for proofreading.

I could not have written this book without my son, Josh, and thank him for his inspiration and magic carpet rides. Unending thanks go out to my husband Pete for making me laugh every day, which has to be some sort of miracle, religious or otherwise.

While essays are one thing, turning them into a book is quite another, and so I am enormously grateful to my brilliant readers Kim Hines, Jorie Latham, Mary Logan, Robert Rees, and Janet Stilson for helping me thread the pieces of this book into the story I wanted to tell.

Thanks are also due to Ellen Byron, whose writing and insights inspire me daily; and to all the friends and family who live in these pages and who brought me from a skittish single mom to a much more confident one. Thank you from every corner of my heart.

JEWISH HOLIDAYS CHEAT SHEET

While this book is by no means a primer on Jewish holidays, I created a cheat sheet in case you want to know more. One thing I did *not* share is pronunciation suggestions. That's because of the story about two Jews who started three synagogues, since they're always disagreeing. Those two will pronounce everything I say differently, and as my father used to say, "I have enough troubles."

The holidays noted here are the ones I chose to write about, those most significant to my personal journey. There are others that have not been included because they aren't part of the book. To learn more about the holidays, you can find numerous sites ranging from Chabad.org to Aish.com to My Jewish Learning to 18 Doors. I recommend you try all of them until you find the one you like best.

The first thing you should know about the Jewish holidays is that they are always changing dates on our Gregorian calendar. That's because the Hebrew calendar is lunar, adjusted to reflect some parts of the solar calendar. While the secular New Year starts on January 1, the Jewish New Year begins in late summer or fall.

Perhaps the best place to start is with Shabbat. I think of it as the very first holiday—and the only one ever celebrated by God.

SHABBAT

The name means Sabbath Day of Rest. Shabbat is celebrated at the end of each week. Shabbat lasts twenty-five hours—from just before sundown on Friday until an hour after sundown on Saturday night. Like most major Jewish holidays, Shabbat begins with lighting candles and blessings over wine and bread. As a child I hated the idea of resting, but as an adult I've come to appreciate it more and more every year.

HIGH HOLY DAYS

The High Holy Days include the Jewish New Year (Rosh Hashanah) and the Day of Atonement (Yom Kippur). The High Holiday season starts a month before Rosh Hashanah and includes the ten days between Rosh Hashanah and Yom Kippur, known as the *Ten Days of Awe*.

ROSH HASHANAH (HEAD OF THE YEAR)

On Rosh Hashanah, Jewish people listen to the sound of the shofar, a ram's horn that signals us to wake up and look closely at our lives and how we live them. It's a time when the Book of Life is supposed to be opened, and when names are either written in it—or not—for the coming year. A family tradition is to eat apples and honey to signify a sweet new year. The most important part of Rosh Hashanah involves trying to repair relationships and apologize for bad behavior during the previous year.

YOM KIPPUR (DAY OF ATONEMENT)

Yom Kippur is a day when Jews over the age of thirteen who are not pregnant or ill/infirm are supposed to fast, pray, and collectively atone as a community. It is said that "on Rosh Hashanah the Book of Life is written, and on Yom Kippur it is sealed."

SUKKOT (BOOTHS)

In ancient times, people made pilgrimages to Jerusalem to celebrate the harvest and pray in the ancient Temple. Rabbinic tradition explains that this week-long holiday commemorates the forty years when the Israelites who escaped Egypt wandered in the desert. To celebrate today, families and communities build a sukkah (house or hut) with three sides and a roof that must still be open to the sky. People eat, socialize, and sometimes sleep in the sukkahs! They can also invite ancestors to join them inside.

SIMCHAT TORAH (HAPPINESS OR REJOICING IN TORAH)

Simchat Torah celebrates the end of reading the year's Torah cycle and starting over again in the new year. This event happens in synagogue, and as soon as the last lines of Torah are read, congregants begin reading it over again from the beginning. The holiday is also celebrated with singing and dancing—and if you're up to it, carrying Torah scrolls around the room while you dance.

HANUKKAH (DEDICATION)

Two words: *Not Christmas.* More words: *candles, potato pancakes, jelly donuts,* and *miracles.* Hanukkah is an eight-day holiday celebrating the Jewish recapture and rededication of the Holy Temple in Jerusalem. The miracle was said to have happened after the Jews threw the conquering army out of the Temple. They had only enough oil to last one night, but the oil burned for eight. People celebrating now light candles enclosed in candelabras called menorahs, which increase from one candle to eight as the holiday goes on.

TU B'SHEVAT (FIFTEENTH OF HEBREW MONTH OF SHEVAT)

When the Temple in Jerusalem was still standing, Jews offered the first fruits of their trees. It is celebrated as the birthday of trees.

PURIM (LOTS)

The Purim story is about a hero named Esther. She saved her people after agreeing to marry a non-Jewish king and letting him know his advisor Haman was plotting genocide. On Purim, Jews dress in costume and read from the Book of Esther, sounding groggers that drown out Haman's name when it's mentioned. Triangular cookies, called *hamantashen*, are supposed to have been created to symbolize Haman's hat.

PASSOVER (PASS OVER)

This holiday lasts eight days and celebrates how God brought the Jewish people out of slavery in Egypt. The name refers to the angel of death *passing over* slaves' houses the night before they fled. Because they had no time to bake while getting ready to leave Egypt, we eat matzah, which is unleavened bread. Luckily, there are thousands of non-Jewish students all over the country who *like* eating matzah, and many Jewish children (like I was) who are all too happy to let them.

YOM HASHOAH—(HOLOCAUST REMEMBRANCE DAY)

The holiday was created to remember the six million Jews who died during the Holocaust and honor those who resisted. Many Jewish communities create commemorative memorial events and light candles for the people who perished.

SHAVUOT (FEAST OF WEEKS)

Shavuot is celebrated seven weeks after Passover. It combines two holidays—the giving of Torah at Mount Sinai to mark the covenant between God and the Jewish people, seven weeks after the exodus from Egypt—and the early summer grain harvest. It is a tradition to stay up all night during the holiday studying Torah.

TISHA B'AV (NINTH OF AV)

The Hebrew name means the ninth day of the Hebrew month of Av. This day is the most mournful of all the holidays, recalling the Roman destruction of the First and Second Temples in Jerusalem. Tisha B'Av is a fasting day, when the Book of Lamentations is chanted in synagogues by congregants who sit in the dark.

BRIT

The Jewish ceremony in which a baby boy is circumcised is called a Brit in Hebrew. Circumcision is first mentioned in the Book of Genesis, when God commands Abraham to circumcise himself and his male children as a sign of the covenant between God and the Jewish people. It is typically performed on the baby's eighth day of life. If medical issues are present, the brit will be postponed until the baby is healthy enough.

MEZUZAH

A mezuzah is a piece of parchment contained in a decorative case and inscribed with specific Hebrew verses from the Torah. These verses consist of the Jewish prayer Shema Yisrael, beginning with the phrase, "Hear, O Israel, the Lord our God, the Lord is One."

MINYAN

A minyan is the minimum number of adult Jews aged thirteen and older who can congregate to fulfill liturgical requirements, such as saying certain prayers like the Mourner's Kaddish. The number required for a minyan is ten.

MIKVEH (RITUAL BATH)

First of all, it's complicated. Jewish law requires that if you are converting to the faith, you immerse yourself completely in the mikveh. Women use the ritual bath before marriage and during marriage after menstruating. My first widely produced play was about the mikveh ritual—and that's all I'm going to say at this point.

TAHARA

This practice was completely unknown to me growing up but has become one of the traditions I treasure most. Tahara involves preparing the deceased for a Jewish burial by ritually washing and dressing the body. The ritual allows those who perform it to share one last act of kindness with the deceased, offering him or her the respect and dignity we all deserve.